Trans Men in the South

Breaking Boundaries

Series Editor: J. E. Sumerau, University of Tampa

Breaking Boundaries is meant to expand the horizons of mainstream and academic understandings of sex, gender, and sexualities. While the last few decades have witnessed increased attention to some areas of sex, gender, and sexualities, mainstream and academic focus has been generally limited to focus on cissex males and females, cisgender women and men, monosexual gay/lesbian/straight, and monogamous individuals, groups, and experiences. Building on the groundwork laid by these traditions, Breaking Boundaries focuses on other arenas of sex, gender, and sexual identities, practices, relationships, experiences, and inequalities too often missing from existing mainstream and academic discussions of sex, gender, and sexualities.

Christianity and the Limits of Minority Acceptance in America: God Loves (Almost) Everyone by J. E. Sumerau and Ryan T. Cragun
Trans Men in the South: Becoming Men by Baker A. Rogers

Trans Men in the South

Becoming Men

Baker A. Rogers

LEXINGTON BOOKS
Lanham • Boulder • New York • London

Published by Lexington Books
Lexington Books is an imprint of The Rowman & Littlefield Publishing Group, Inc.
4501 Forbes Boulevard, Suite 200, Lanham, Maryland 20706
www.rowman.com

6 Tinworth Street, London SE11 5AL, United Kingdom

British Library Cataloguing in Publication Information Available

Library of Congress Cataloging-in-Publication Data

Library of Congress Control Number:2019956728

ISBN 978-1-7936-0033-2 (cloth)
ISBN 978-1-7936-0035-6 (paperback)
ISBN 978-1-7936-0034-9 (electronic)

Contents

Preface

In this book, I examine the lives of 51 trans men across the Southeastern United States. As a queer, Southern, feminist sociologist, I approach this project from a position within the Southern trans community, which gives me a unique perspective to understand the experiences of trans men in the South. Like many of the trans men in this study, I see myself as an "outsider-within" the South (Collins 2000). While I have some identities of privilege that allow me to "claim sameness," such as being white and from the rural Southeast, I also have other identities that clearly mark me as an outsider, such as not identifying as religious and identifying as a genderqueer lesbian. My personal connections with the queer community in the Southeast allowed me to gain access to different networks of queer people and to gain the trust of my respondents. My insider position in the queer community gives me access to trans men who may be hesitant to speak with other researchers for fear of how their lives will be portrayed. To date, most academics who have studied trans men do not identify as trans themselves.

Despite my positionality, as a genderqueer Southerner, I'm also still learning and educating myself on the changing meaning of gender in our society. For instance, like Travers (2018, 9), I prefer "they/them/their" pronouns for myself, yet I continue to get it wrong sometimes. For most of us, binary gender pronouns are ingrained, and the use of "they/them/their" as singular pronouns is a relatively recent development. Language changes quickly, and we all must try to keep up for the safety and well-being of everyone. Therefore, I'm going to take a moment to explain the language I use in this book, in this specific sociopolitical moment.

LANGUAGE AS A TOOL OF POWER

It is important to understand the terminology I am using in this book and the power of language and discourse as tools. Language, like any socially constructed system of meaning, holds power (for more, see Foucault 1978; 1980). It is my intention in this book to use the language of my respondents to the best of my ability; however, it must be noted that everyone in our society is influenced by an incomplete system of words and ideas. Also, language is not constant. Sometimes changes occur slowly, and sometimes, as is the current case with language around gender and sexuality in our society, language changes faster than the pace of publishing. My aim is to use the most accurate and inclusive language I can, but if my language and terminology is found to be lacking or exclusive after publication, I hope you, the reader, will update this language in your understanding of my findings and in your future work in this field. This book marks a specific moment in the evolution of language, and our understanding of gender and sexuality is far from complete. Despite this, outdated or inappropriate language can be disrespectful and damaging; therefore, it is the scholar's ethical responsibility to do their best to use the most up-to-date language and to be transparent about the choices we have made. On that note, let me explain some of my choices of terminology to guide you through this book and give you an introduction to gender and sexuality if you are unfamiliar with the field.

First, we must distinguish between sex, gender, and sexuality. While these concepts are often used interchangeably and are highly interconnected, understanding the distinctions between these concepts allows for a more complete understanding of people who fall outside of the gender and sexual binaries in our culture. Sex generally refers to the biological characteristics used to divide humans into categories—usually male and female. These include, but are not limited to, genitalia, hormones, and chromosomes. While sex is based on these biological makers, it is also a social construction. These biological markers can, and do, shift over time and do not always neatly align with the binary sex system of male/female. For instance, intersexuality encompasses an array of differences that can lead someone's body to not fit neatly into one of the two categories we have created. To learn more about sex and intersexuality, which this book touches on but does not deeply analyze, see Georgiann Davis' work, including their recent book *Contesting Intersex: The Dubious Diagnosis* (2015).

A related, but separate category of classification and identity is gender. Gender encompasses the social expectations we place on people, usually based on their assumed sex category (West and Zimmerman 1987). In doing gender theory, sex category is the sex a person is assumed to be by others in interaction, usually based on secondary sexual characteristics (e.g., breasts, an Adam's apple, or facial hair), while gender describes how a person performs masculinity and femininity in interaction with others, and how this performance is judged by others. Sex, sex category, and gender are not ahistorical facts; rather they are social constructs that vary depending on the situation and time. Starting before birth, people place gendered expectations on children and socialize them into the expected behaviors and presentations thought to be appropriate for the gender we presume they will be based on an ultrasound of the fetus. Once the child is born, they are taught to "act like a girl" or "act like a boy"; to "do gender" in a way that aligns with the sex they were assigned at birth (West and Zimmerman 1987). Gender does not come naturally; rather, it is taught, and then heavily policed and enforced by society. As West and Zimmerman (1987; 2009) explain, whether people follow the rules of gender or not, they are always held accountable to acting in a way that aligns with their assumed sex, their sex category.

Gender performance or expression is about how masculine, feminine, both, or neither a person appears to be and behaves. While the characteristics associated with masculinity and femininity shift over time and place, they seem to most people to be inevitable and essential to human beings. Today in the United States, masculinity is generally defined as strength, aggressiveness, and power. Femininity is almost always defined in opposition to masculinity. It is everything masculinity is not: weakness, gentleness, and inferiority. While these concepts are difficult to define, most people know them when they see them. Also, when people choose not to do gender, or cannot do gender in the expected way, others hold them accountable for breaking these norms through shaming, and sometimes violence.

Most of the men in this study "do masculinity" and hold certain ideas about what it means to be a man in our society. R. Connell (2009a) uses the concept of multiple masculinities. They explain that all men do not gain benefits equally from being recognized as men, or doing masculinity. At the top of the hierarchy in the U.S., receiving the most benefits and privileges from masculinity—what R. Connell (2009a) calls the "patriarchal dividend"—are white, cisgender, heterosexual, Christian men. This is what Connell labels hegemonic masculinity—the currently dominant form of masculinity in a culture at a specific time and location. Masculinities that still receive patriarchal dividends, but to a lesser degree, include marginalized masculinities (men of color; poor men); subordinated masculinities (gay men); and complicit masculinities (men who do not actively participate in the domination of women, but are complicit in and receive benefits from the domination) (R. Connell 2009a). In contrast to masculinity, femininity is never hegemonic because it is always defined and performed in relation and subordination to masculinity in our society.

Finally, sexuality refers to attraction, both sexual and romantic. Sexuality does not neatly flow from sex and gender, as most of us were taught. One may be sexually attracted to the same sex or gender (lesbian, gay, queer, etc.), romantically attracted to the opposite sex or gender (heteroromantic), or not attracted to anyone sexually (asexual) or romantically (aromantic); the list of possible sexualities and combinations of sex/gender/sexuality is endless. Not all men in this study are attracted to women. Some of the men I spoke with are attracted to other men, some are attracted to people regardless of gender expression or identity, and still others are not sexually attracted to anyone.

Trans/transgender can be either an umbrella term or an individual identity. The commonality among these identities is that the person does not identify with the sex they were assigned at birth in some way. Cisgender, in contrast to transgender, refers to a person whose gender identity aligns with the sex they were assigned at birth (i.e., a person assigned female at birth who identifies as a woman, or a person assigned male at birth who identifies as a man). All of the interviewees identified as trans masculine in some form. I use the term "trans men" throughout the book to refer to the variety of individual identities of the respondents who were all assigned female sex at birth based on an interpretation of their biology, but who now identify their sex as male, their gender as man, and/or their gender expression as masculine. While there is no agreed upon label for this population, trans men or trans masculine best encompasses the commonalities among respondents. Additionally, all of the interviewees self-selected into a study for trans men. The call for interviewees read: "Participants in this study must be at least 18 years of age; identify as a transgender man, transmale, transman, female-to-male (FTM), male or man (who was assigned female at birth), or some other identity that signifies transition from female to male; and currently live in the Southeastern United States." Notice that the words "trans" and "men" are separated with a space, because trans does not encompass the whole of these respondents' identities. Trans is but one aspect of who they are as a person—an adjective that describes them. This is why you never see "whitemen" or "gaymen" written as single words. In the same way, trans should be used as an adjective to describe an identity.

Finally, regarding terminology in this book, I use "queer" to refer broadly to individuals who identify with non-normative genders and sexualities. This term replaces concepts like LGBTQIA+ (which stands for lesbian, gay, bisexual, trans, queer, intersex, and ally, plus) in order to be as inclusive as possible. The term "queer" includes those who identify with accepted categories of identity in our society (such as gay, lesbian, bisexual, transgender, etc.), but also includes those "whose identities may not be easily classified using other identity terms or categories" (Pfeffer 2017, xxxv). Therefore, in this study, queer is an inclusive term for all individuals whose genders and sexualities do not neatly fit into the hetero-cisnormative framework of our society. That is, the assumption that everyone is male (sex), man (gender), and heterosexual (sexuality), *or* female (sex), woman (gender), and heterosexual (sexuality). As previously stated, all labels are contested and constantly shifting, and so not all respondents choose the term "queer," or other terms I use in this study, for their own identities. Therefore, when I discuss specific respondents, I provide their gender identity and sexuality in their own terms. For reference and ease of reading, I have included a table of terms and definitions that appear throughout the book.

Table Preface.1. Terminology

Term	Definition
Bi+	Sexual and/or romantic attraction to more than one sex/gender or regardless of sex/gender; including, but not limited to, pansexual, bisexual, queer, etc.; an umbrella term for anyone who does not identify as monosexual
Biphobia	Systematic oppression of people who are sexually or romantically attracted to more than one sex/gender
Cisgender/Cis	A person whose gender identity aligns with the sex they were assigned at birth; i.e., a person assigned female at birth identifies as a woman or a person assigned male at birth identifies as a man
Cisnormativity	The assumption that everyone's gender identity matches the sex they were assigned at birth; promotes the idea that there are only two sexes and genders
Cissexism	Discrimination against and oppression of trans and gender non-binary people based on the idea that cisgender identities are better or more normal than trans identities
Drag king	Any person (regardless of sex or gender identity) who performs masculinity within the context of a drag show or contest
Gender	The social expectations placed on people, usually based on their assumed sex category; a socially constructed spectrum of masculinity and femininity
Gender binary	The idea that there are only two types of people—male-bodied people who are masculine and identify as men and female-bodied people who are feminine and identify as women
Gender identity	A sense of oneself as man, woman, trans, genderqueer, gender non-binary, etc.
Heteronormativity	The assumption that everyone is heterosexual until proven otherwise; the belief that heterosexuality is better or more normal than same-sex attraction or desire
Heterosexism	Discrimination against and oppression of sexual minorities, including gay, lesbian, bi+, asexual, etc.
Homonormativity	A hierarchy among sexual minorities valuing those who conform to cis- and heterosexist institutions and norms

(continued)

Table Preface.1. (*continued*)

Term	Definition
Homophobia	Systematic oppression of people who are sexually or romantically attracted to the same sex/gender
Monosexual	Sexual and/or romantic attraction to only one sex or gender; usually refers to people who identify as gay, lesbian, or heterosexual; also refers to people who prefer one partner at a time, such as people who are monogamous
Non-binary	A gender identity or expression for those who do not identify as only "man" or "woman"; can include genderqueer, agender, gender non-conforming, etc.; those who identify as non-binary may or may not identify as trans or under the trans umbrella
Passing	To be read by others as the gender one identities with, rather than the sex assigned at birth
Queer	Inclusive term for individuals who identify with non-normative genders and sexualities, including, but not limited to, lesbian, gay, bisexual, transgender, asexual, pansexual, genderqueer, non-binary, etc.; used as an umbrella term for a community of people who do not identify with the gender and sexual binaries that can be used to replace the various iterations of LGBTQIA+ and be more inclusive; not always a label that various members of this community are comfortable with individually
Rape	Forced oral, anal, or vaginal sexual penetration by a body part or object
Sex	The biological characteristics used to divide humans into categories of male and female; also includes intersex—people whose biological characteristics do not neatly align with the biological markers used to assign sex; a socially constructed spectrum of expected bodily characteristics that are used to place one into a male or female category
Sexual assault	Unwanted sexual contact, including, but not limited to, touching and fondling; sometimes used synonymously with rape, but sexual assault stops short of attempted/completed rape
Sexual harassment	Unwelcome sexual advances, requests for sexual favors, or other verbal or physical harassment of a sexual nature
Sexuality	A person's sexual attractions and behaviors; includes sexual identities, such as lesbian, gay, pansexual, bisexual, polysexual, etc.
Trans men	Variety of identities of individuals who were assigned female at birth based on an interpretation of biology (sex), but who identify their sex as male, their gender as man, and/or their gender expression as masculine
Transgender/Trans	A person whose gender identity does not align with the sex they were assigned at birth; can be an identity or an umbrella category

Term	Definition
Transnormativity	The pressure for trans people to fit a cisgender presentation of what it means to be a man or woman; creates a hierarchy of transness based on appearance and physical transitions
Transphobia	Systematic oppression of people who do not identify with the gender that aligns with the sex they were assigned at birth

Note: I wrote these definitions for this specific study. They combine a number of resources and more information about each can be found by using the index to refer to the terms where they appear in the book and to the references for this book. Importantly, definitions and concepts are continuously changing and vary based on time and social location. Therefore, these definitions are for the purposes of understanding this work and the respondents who shared their stories with me in the current context and time, specifically in the Southeastern United States in the late 2010s.

Acknowledgments

First, I would like to thank my family and friends for their continued support and encouragement. Most importantly, I want to thank my wife, Sarah, who supports me in everything I do and who helped me to edit this book. I want to thank Georgia Southern University for the generous research start-up funds, as well as the Scholarly Pursuit Award that funded this project. Thank you to Megan Phillips, my fearless graduate assistant, who assisted with recruitment, transcribed many of the interviews in this study, and completed endless hours of grading so I could work on this book. Keep an eye out for Megan as a rising star in sociology. Thank you to Courtney Lachapelle Morales, my editor at Lexington Books, and to J. E. Sumerau, the series editor for Breaking Boundaries: New Horizons in Gender & Sexuality. It has been a pleasure working with you both on this project, and I am proud to be among the books in this special series with J. Thank you to the anonymous reviewers who helped me improve the quality of this book for publication and to the copyediting team for making me sound even better. Finally, thank you to the trans men across the Southeastern United States who trusted me enough to share their stories with me. I hope that you find this book a fair representation of your story, and a helpful resource for those who wish to educate themselves about our lives as queer people in the South.

Introduction

The United States is a long way from being an accepting society that allows trans people to live authentically and without fear. While increased acceptance and visibility over the last decade has changed the landscape for trans men in the United States, the Southeastern United States (henceforth referred to as the South or Southeast) remains socially and politically behind in accepting queer people (Abelson 2019; Barton 2012; Baunach, Burgess, and Muse 2010; Sumerau and Cragun 2018). The heightened heteronormativity and transphobia in the South (Bradford et al. 2013; Mathers, Sumerau, and Cragun 2018) leaves many trans men feeling the need to fit into the gender expectations of the region. This book is for trans people, and is hopefully a step in the direction of acceptance in the Southeast, where change and acceptance always seem a little slower to take hold than in other regions of the country. As Jazz Jennings (2016), LGBTQ activist and one of the youngest trans people in the national spotlight, explains, "Progress can't happen just from trans people being out in the open. Society also has to truly accept transgender individuals. If society is capable of treating us equally, then we can and will live authentically. And that acceptance starts here with all of us now."

"I identify as a, I guess it would be, I dunno, heterosexual male, but I am trans male, if that makes sense. . . . I'm not stealth, in that I don't hide the fact that I'm trans, I call it stealth in that unless somebody asks me, like nobody would know. I'm completely under the trans radar." Meet Nolan[1], a 36-year-old straight white trans male, who had lived his entire life in the Southeast in a "very small rural backwoods town in Arkansas." At the time of his interview, he lived in Georgia, in a town he described as a "suburb-like, suburban small town; it's not near as retro minded as the place I grew up, but . . . it's still a small town mentality." While Nolan did not want to hide his trans identity, he felt that to live authentically in the Southeast meant he would have to be recognized as a man, not a trans man. Unlike some other respondents, Nolan was willing to tell people about his trans identity if they ask, but otherwise he was happy living "under the trans radar" where he is safe and accepted among those with a "small town mentality."

Like Nolan, Colton also flew under the radar in the South: "I feel there's a push to identify as trans, because I think some people want the limelight and they want to be seen; which, being seen isn't the problem, but there's some of us who, like me and my job, need to fly under the radar, more so." Colton, a 28-year-old straight white trans man, also lived his whole life in the Southeast. He was born in North Carolina, but raised and spent the majority of his life in suburban South Carolina. As a firefighter and EMT, Colton said his job is too important and he doesn't have time to deal with his trans identity in the heat of the moment; it is easier if people assume he is a cis man and he can just do his job.

When I asked Leo how long he'd lived in the Southeast, he said, "I've actually done the math. It's approximate—well, almost half of my life actually. Probably 15 years." Leo, who identified as an African American straight male, had lived in suburban North Carolina since 2011. For Leo, being recognized as a man was important for his family's safety: "Just because a lot of people around here are very conservative. And so it has to be stealth. For me, it's for my kids' sake. I am very happy that my middle son is graduating because that means all the parents that knew me before [transition] will no longer—I no longer have to associate with them, so I don't have to explain anything." Leo specifically pointed to his understanding of living in the South, in a very conservative area, as a reason to stay under the radar. He didn't feel he could be open about being trans and was happy that most of the people who knew he was trans would soon no longer be a part of his life.

Finally, Walker had lived in rural Tennessee for 25 years, almost exactly half of his life. At 51, he identified as a white bisexual male and also saw the value in staying below the trans radar: "I just kinda wanna fly under the radar. Just kinda pass and if that is possible that's the way I'm just gonna identify from here on out, is I'd prefer I'm a man." For better or worse, trans men in the Southeast often live their lives under the radar. Many "pass" as cisgender men, while others are read as butch or masculine women. While being a masculine woman is still not generally accepted in our society, it is more tolerated in the South, particularly the rural South, than being trans or a feminine man. For those trans men recognized as cis men, passing confers privileges that is often unobtainable for trans women. However, passing as cisgender also leads to problems of invisibility in the queer community, which is already small and often hidden in this region of the country. In this book, I examine trans men in the Southeast and the privileges and vulnerabilities that come with these identities. While being a man garners respect and power in our society, most trans men in the South live in constant fear of being discovered and forced to face the discrimination and violence that may follow.

Through the voices of 51 trans men across the Southeast, I provide a glimpse into various aspects of what it means to be a trans man in the region. As with any identity, there is no universal experience, but there are common themes that pervade in specific geographic locations. These commonalities are always complicated by other intersecting identities, such as sexuality, religion, race, class, and place; therefore, I take an intersectional perspective to examine how trans masculine identities in the South intersect with these other identities. The goal of this book is to allow the reader to gain a more complete and nuanced understanding of a group that is often invisible—by choice or necessity. Like Sumerau and Mathers (2019, 5), in their recent book *America Through Transgender Eyes*, I argue that "shifting the focus from cisgender assumptions and norms to insights gleaned from transgender experience offers an opportunity to revise and transform not only social scientific studies of gender, but also our understanding of religion, medical science, research methodologies, and LGBTQIA experiences in society." In sharing the perspectives of trans men in the South, my hope is that by experiencing the full humanity of this understudied population, people will become more accepting and empathetic. I hope that the South can rise above the close-minded stereotypes of the region to see trans men, and all people, as human and deserving of respect and inclusion in our diverse world.

INTERSECTIONALITY AND TRANS MASCULINITIES

How trans men do gender intersects with their other identities, such as sexuality, race, class, nationality, ability, and more. Crenshaw (1989) introduced the concept of intersectionality to demonstrate the influence of race on the various experiences of women, and specifically black women. Intersectionality complicates the notion that studying gender alone is sufficient for understanding inequality. The intersectional approach moves scholars beyond adding oppressions to the consideration of unique standpoints within the matrix of domination (Collins 1986; 2009) and how these distinct standpoints create unique experiences for people—socially, politically, and economically (Holvino 2010; Collins 1986; 2009). Intersectionality theory also demonstrates how geographic location changes the meanings of these varying characteristics and their relationships to inequality (Glenn 2002; Mohanty 2003). As Abelson (2019, 8) reveals, understanding the influence of geographic location on men's lives is as important as understanding other intersecting characteristics.

Around the same time that the concept of intersectionality was being formu-
lated within black and multiracial feminism, R. Connell proposed a theory of
multiple masculinities, which posits that all masculine identities are not equal
and that hegemonic masculinity is not stable (Abelson 2019; R. Connell 2009).
This theory makes clear that intersections of other privileges and oppressions
such as race, class, or sexuality can lessen the power and resources available
to certain men. Based on this theory, all men are striving for hegemonic masculinity, which is "the currently most honored way of being a man, required all
other men to position themselves in relation to it, and ideologically legitimated
the global subordination of women to men" (R. Connell and Messerschmidt
2005, 832). However, despite multiple masculinities theories complicating our
notion of a static form of masculinity, the theories largely continue to limit
masculinities to male bodies (Abelson 2019; Halberstam 1998).

One study that examined masculinities and how they intersect with other
identities outside of bodies assigned male at birth was Schilt's (2006) study
of trans men in the workplace. Schilt (2006) found that in the workplace race
and ethnicity had a negative influence on the privileges trans men received.
Experiences of trans men of color in the workplace were very different from
white trans men's experiences; men of color evoked different racial stereotypes which tempered the privileges of masculinity. Other studies of trans
men also point to the importance of intersectionality. In their 2013 study,
Rowniak and Chesla found that for trans men in San Francisco, the idea of
transitioning and then identifying as straight did not make sense; heterosexual
men "represented a community and way of being that were both foreign
and unappealing for all" (458). Along the same lines, Catalano (2015, 422)
found that for trans men in college in New England, being recognized as cis
men was problematic: "For some, the experience of being categorized with
cisgender men raised the question of whether their masculine postures reified
normative masculinity." Finally, in a nationwide sample of 42 transgender
people who identified as heterosexual, Sumerau et al. (2018, 8) found that
most participants "defined cisgender assumptions and norms as too limiting,
and incapable of capturing their experiences."

Abelson (2016a; 2019), one of the few scholars who has used masculinities
theories to examine the lives of trans men at the intersections of identity and
geographic location, finds that some trans men are able to gain acceptance
through claims of sameness, in terms of race, class, and sexuality, with other
men in the region. Specifically, trans men are more likely to feel safe and
accepted within their communities when they can claim sameness through
white, rural, working-class, heterosexual masculinity. Other trans men who
cannot claim sameness are unable to garner acceptance and gain access to the
privileges of masculinity in some way. And even trans men who could gain

such privileges, including "reprieve from the social stigma and potential danger of ambiguous gender expression, as well as access to social and material resources granted only to particular group members," understand that these privileges can be taken away at any time if people realize the men are not cis, heterosexual, or like them in other ways (Pfeffer 2017, 39). The likelihood of having one's access and reprieve revoked is intensified in the South, which makes it especially important to understand trans men's intersections of identity in this region of the country.

THE SOUTH: THE IMPORTANCE OF LOCATION

In this study, I examine a region of the country where "yes ma'am" and "yes sir" prevail. A region where "What church do you go to?" and "Who's your family?" defines you more than any individual characteristic, career, or hobby. The Southeast remains a place where everything is gendered; from our language, to our extravagant gender reveal parties (see Guignard 2015) and baby showers, to the religious services the majority of Southerners still attend on Sunday mornings.

In fact, gender is so present and presumed that some of the trans men misgendered me during their interview. Despite my masculine-sounding name (Baker) and the topic of this study (trans men), some of the respondents felt it necessary or polite to call me "ma'am" during our phone interviews, based on my feminine voice. This demonstrates how difficult it is to live outside of gendered assumptions in a society that has so fully institutionalized gender into our language, discourses, organizations, and policies. This also foreshadows my discussion of how issues of transphobia, homophobia, heterosexism, etc. are not exclusive concerns of cisgender and heterosexual people. As I will discuss more fully in Chapter 6, misunderstandings, discrimination, and oppression also pervade the queer community, which is certainly not immune to the influences of a cis- and heteronormative society.

The Southeastern United States, often referred to as the South, is the region of the country south of the Mason-Dixon Line. The South includes the eleven ex-Confederate, slave states, plus Kentucky and Oklahoma (Mazzuca 2002; Reed 1986). Today, over 150 years after the official end of legal racial discrimination in the South, the legacy of racism remains a defining feature of the South. In addition to race, the South is defined by political and social conservatism, both in regard to politics and religion. Based on the conservatism of the region, it should not be surprising that gender and sexuality are also constructed in largely binary and limiting ways. The Southeast remains a geographic location where gender is omnipresent and stereotypical displays of masculinity are expected.

In the Southeast, research demonstrates increased levels of homophobia (Barton 2012; Baunach, Burgess, and Muse 2010), biphobia (Mathers, Sumerau, and Cragun 2018), and transphobia (Bradford et al. 2013; Mathers et al. 2018), largely due to conservative religious and political ideology. While some scholars have documented a slow decline in prejudice and discrimination against gay cis men and lesbian cis women, other gender and sexual minorities do not appear to be benefiting to the same degree from the advancement of gay and lesbian civil rights and acceptance (Cragun and Sumerau 2015; Mathers et al. 2018; Sumerau, Grollman, and Cragun 2018). As some religious communities begin to be more accepting of lesbian cis women and gay cis men, they continue to ostracize trans people, bisexual people, and people who are not monogamous. Furthermore, not all religious communities are opening their doors to queers to any degree. For instance, in my book *Conditionally Accepted: Christians' Perspectives on Sexuality & Gay and Lesbian Civil Rights* (2019b), I find that despite close friends or family members who identify as gay or lesbian, Southern evangelical Protestants are not changing their beliefs and opinions about homosexuality or gay and lesbian civil rights. So, even as progress is being made and more people than ever in the United States are supportive of queer rights, there are still groups who face strong opposition and groups who do not seem to be moving towards acceptance or equality of queer people in any way. Despite slow social change regarding queer people, and even slower change with respect to trans people, there remains a vibrant and thriving queer culture in the Southeast, even in rural areas often ignored by scholars (Abelson 2016a; Barton 2012; Stone 2018). In fact, over a third of queer people in the United States reside in the Southeast (Stone 2018).

To date, the majority of research on queer life has been conducted in "urban enclaves" outside of the Southeast, in cities such as San Francisco and New York (Stone 2018). The lack of research in the South, in rural areas and "ordinary cities" in particular, has led to a metronormative narrative of queer life (Kazyak 2012; Stone 2019). For instance, in one of the first comprehensive looks at trans men in the United States, Rubin (2003) studies men in San Francisco, Boston, and New York. Rubin (2003, 4) acknowledged that the men he studied "may be different from FTMs [female-to-male] in rural, inland areas that lack anonymity, medical specialists, or community support." Indeed they are. Yet, as of 2019 there is still relatively little research that examines trans, and queer life more generally, in the South, in rural areas, or in "ordinary cities." As Stone (2018, 2) argues, "This metronormative narrative contributes to the construction of gay life as a White, urban, upper-middle class phenomenon."

The current understanding of queer life, especially within sociological literature, largely ignores the experiences of trans people in the South. While over a third of queer people in the United States live in the South, only one in ten sociology studies examining queer life focuses on the South as a location of study (Stone 2018). Consequently, more research is needed to understand the experiences of queer people, especially transgender people, in the Southeast. This study answers the call for more such analysis. While some of the respondents lived in moderately-sized cities in the Southeast, only four respondents lived in Atlanta, Georgia, the only city somewhat comparable to the "great cities" of the United States where most research on queer life has been conducted (Stone 2018). The majority of the respondents resided in small, ordinary cities or rural areas. Moreover, this study illustrates the issues with a metronormative narrative of queer life by exploring queer life among diverse racial groups and socioeconomic classes (largely working-class respondents), and in rural areas.

This oversight in the study of queer lives is even more egregious when we consider that "almost 97 percent of territory [in the United States] . . . remains nonurbanized, or 'rural,' in character" (Johnson, Gilley, and Gray 2016, 1). The Southeast is a unique geographic location, both in reality and in the national imagination. This is especially true when considering the intersections of Southern life and rural living. By ignoring the South and rural areas, people can continue to view these areas through a uniform lens which tells them that all Southerners and people who live in rural areas are conservative—religiously, politically, and socially; that people in these regions are mostly Christian; and that all Southerners are closed-minded (Johnson et al. 2016). Whether these stereotypes of the South and rural areas are true or not (some are, but most are exaggerated), they influence beliefs about queer lives in these areas of the country. These beliefs lead to the persistent view that queer people leave the South and rural areas for urban enclaves as soon as possible (Kazyak 2012); however, this perspective completely ignores the demographic evidence about where queer people are actually living their lives. It also ignores the diversity of queer people's beliefs, cultures, and goals. As Kazyak (2012) demonstrates in her article "Midwest or Lesbian? Gender, Rurality, and Sexuality," not all queer people desire to leave rural areas. Likewise, Abelson (2019) found that many trans men have made their lives in the Southeast and in rural areas and intend to stay there.

In opposition to the metronormative narrative dominant in queer studies, the men in this study described where they grew up and where they lived as country, small town, or rural. One interviewee, Jamar, a 30-year-old white pansexual male, said, "I lived a lot of my life in the country. I was out in the middle of bumfuck Egypt." Another respondent, Mason, a 34-year-old Indigenous two-spirit queer person who lived in Tennessee, most clearly debunked the metronormative narrative of queer life. For Mason, the idea that queer people should, or do, run to the cities at the first opportunity doesn't make sense, much like for the lesbians in Kazyak's (2012) study. Mason lived "thirty miles from the nearest anything" and having lived almost his entire life in the South, he explained,

> I think that we tend to make our homes in places where we blend more with the culture than not. So, like me with my cowboy boots, jeans, and cowboy hat, I don't fit in an urban area. Stick out like a sore thumb. . . . Somebody wearin' stilettos going out on the farm is gonna stick out like a sore thumb, too. So, I find that I fit and belong more in these rural areas, than I do in a city setting.

The idea that queer people stick out in the South is based on stereotypes about what queer people look and act like. Just like cis and heterosexual people, queer people differ based on their personalities and cultures.

Brown's (2017, 10) work on the history of sex (sexual intercourse, not biological sex) in the South shows how stereotypes and discourses have shaped this region of the country; the "common assertion about the South holds that old-fashioned or retrograde or repressive notions about women and sexuality persisted longer there than they did in other parts of the country." This assertation is based in some reality as Southern states were some of the last to decriminalize consensual same-sex sexuality. In fact, most Southern states did not *choose* to decriminalize consensual same-sex sexuality; rather their laws were ruled unconstitutional in 2003 when a Supreme Court ruling, *Lawrence v. Texas*, made same-sex sex legal across the country. As late as 2014, the Louisiana State House voted to reject a repeal of their anti-sodomy law that still remains on the books, even though it was ruled unconstitutional a decade earlier (The Associated Press 2014). However, this does not mean that the South is opposed to sex and sexuality, but that those who mandate a specific type of heterosexual sex—monogamous sex between a married man and woman—have been louder within the conversation throughout the last century in the South.

According to Brown (2017, 18), "What has mattered and continues to matter is the fact that sex and sexualities shape and are shaped by a culture that has been . . . an oppositional culture for significant parts of the twentieth and early twenty-first centuries, thus accounting in part for some perceptions that the region is puritanical and not sex-friendly." This perception is directly related to the religious nature, particularly evangelical Protestantism, of the region. The "intense religiosity of much of the South has made sex a site of guilt, and not a pleasurable guilt that comes with the satisfaction of pushing back against cultural constraints" (19). Many Southern Christians, especially conservative Christians, have continued to mount resistance to any type of sexuality that falls outside of the heterosexual norms (Rogers 2019b). Overall, Brown concludes that "the South has trended conservative on most of the major issues of sex and sexuality that admit of contest in the political arena" (20). This directly relates to issues of sexual and gender identity in the region.

Many of these conservative notions of sexuality continue today, even among those who identify as gender and sexual minorities. The heteronormativity, homonormativity, and monosexuality (attraction to members of one sex or gender only; 43 percent of respondents identified as monosexual) among trans men in this region of the country are tied to multiple topics that will be explored in this book, including passing, privilege, and religion. Being trans does not make one immune to the religious guilt and ideologies about proper sexuality that prevail in the South. Yet, as Brown (2017, 22) explains, despite heteronormativity and conservative ideals of sexuality in the South, "Southerners have imagined and performed their sexualities, and continue to do so, in a variety of ways."

Overall, the South, rurality, and religion play key roles in trans men's understanding and experiences of gender, sexuality, safety, and desire to pass as cis men. These three elements intersect to create unique experiences for the men in this study. In an area of the country known for stereotypical gender norms (Carter and Borch 2005), the Southeast, particularly in rural areas, is a location where trans identities are not necessarily tied to queerness or a heightened understanding of gender. Space and place are crucial to understanding gender (Abelson 2019; Johnson et al. 2016); therefore, sociologists must "confront their own epistemological assumptions about LGBTQ life, particularly the understanding that the most exciting forms of queer life are in the major cities . . . ask new questions about LGBTQ life in other places and to examine these social forms within their context" (Stone 2018, 10). This book begins to answer this call by talking to trans men across the Southeast. As Travers (2018, 1) explains, "Our biographies are shaped by our lived experience in specific geopolitical and historical moments. Context is not everything, but it certainly counts for a lot."

When I spoke with these men, 23 were living in Georgia, eight in South Carolina, eight in Tennessee, four in Virginia, two in Arkansas, two in Florida, and one each in Kentucky and North Carolina. The remaining two respondents moved outside of the Southeast for school or work after living the majority of their lives in the South. All of the men in this study lived at least one year in the South, with a range of one to 37 years. The average number of years spent in the South was 22. Most of the men (40 of 51) had lived at least half of their lives in the region, and 41 percent (21 of 51) had never lived outside of the Southeast. A quarter of the interviewees (13 of 51) grew up in rural areas, mostly in the Southeast, 19 of the men grew up mainly in the suburbs, and 14 in urban areas. The remaining respondents moved around to various locations growing up, a handful being children of military parents. At the time of our interviews in 2018, approximately 28 percent (14 of 51) of the men described the area they lived in as rural, 17 as suburban, and 20 as urban. As these numbers demonstrate, queer people come from and live in the South and in rural areas, and many choose to stay.

It is important to note that even though many of the trans men I interviewed chose to stay in the South, they understood the potential downfalls of their decision and the stereotypes of the region as close-minded and less than welcoming to gender and sexual minorities. For instance, Bruno, a 23-year-old white polysexual male who lived in South Carolina, explained that he lives in a small city, but "city as it may be, there's a very rural mentality." This idea of rural mentality indicated to him that things may not be safe for a trans man, especially not a polysexual trans man. Later in the interview Bruno discussed this Southern and rural mentality more;

> There's just a very different mentality in the South . . . there's a lot more big-otry here because religion is really deeply tied to the way of life here and that imposes ideas on how people should be. . . . I definitely have gone out of my way to not be visibly trans or visibly queer in any way . . . because we live in the South . . . I think being here does put more pressure on me to be passable. Cause there's just not as much acceptance here.

Though this presumed mentality of the South can make the region feel more dangerous at times, it also allowed trans men to "map out geographies" of fear (Abelson 2019), and most learned to navigate the region in ways that made them feel comfortable. I will discuss this more throughout the book, specifically in Chapter 4, but for now I wish to show that while the Southeast can be a dangerous, or presumed dangerous, area of the country for trans men, it is also an area that most of these men have grown up in and feel most comfortable in. For the majority of men, moving to a big city or another region of the country would lead them to feel just as unsafe, especially since mapping their geographies of fear would be difficult, if not impossible, at first.

Theo grew up in a suburban area in South Carolina, but lived in a much more rural area of South Carolina at the time of his interview. As a young (24 years old) white straight male he felt comfortable in the rural South, but worried about his safety at times. Theo explained, "For me, where I live, it's important that I pass just because it is a rural area, it's a little backwards at times." Theo went on to tell me he wanted to transfer his testosterone pre-

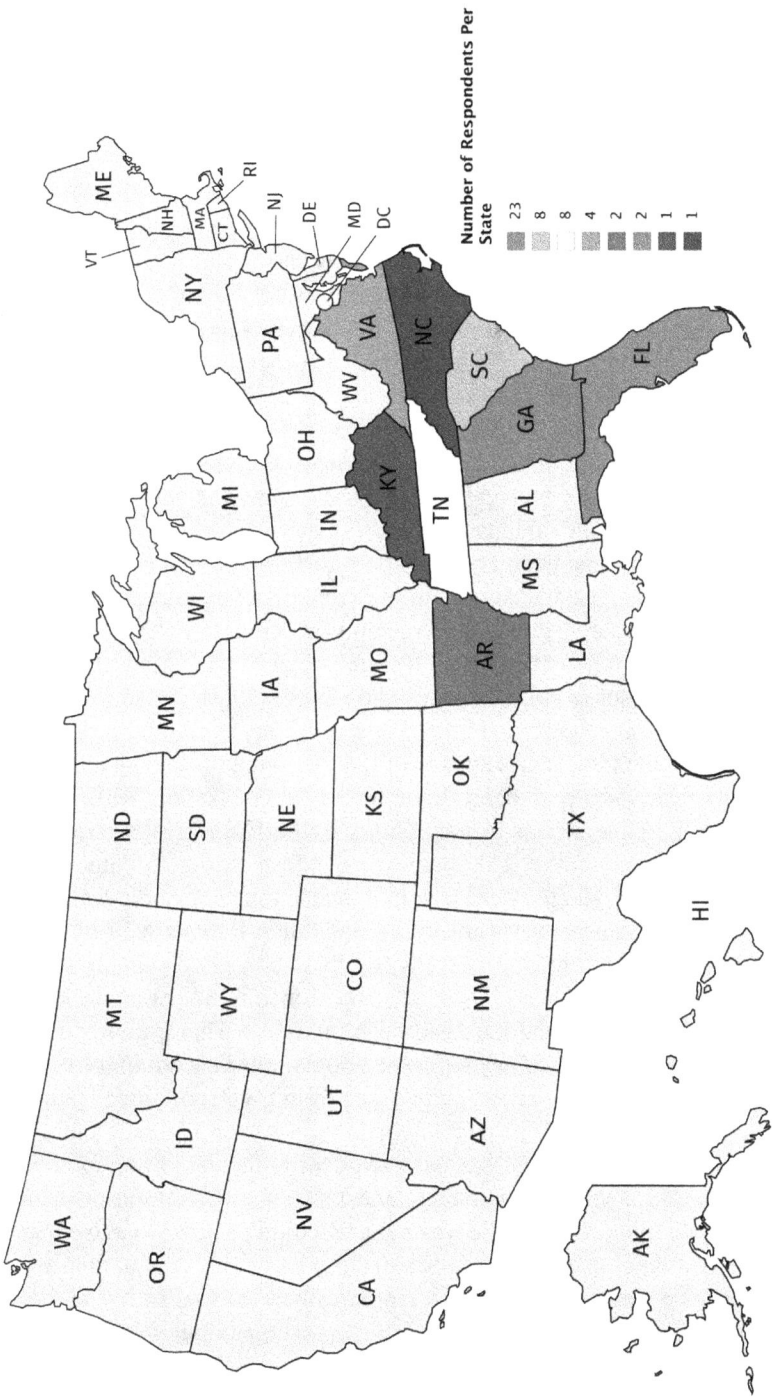

Image of the United States with the eight states represented in the sample highlighted and the number of respondents per state noted. Image created by author.

scription to the local pharmacy, but decided he would rather drive the 20 minutes to the next town. He said it could be dangerous if people found out he's trans, because he works at a gas station in this rural town and has already "had some coworkers that have tried to start some rumors." Overall, Theo said, "I don't really care . . . how people see me, but like I said, living in a rural town, I'm a little more guarded about [being trans]."

Relatedly, Samuel, a 22-year-old white queer trans man from a "real small town" in Kentucky, told me the town he grew up in had less than 10,000 people in it: "So, it's not the smallest . . . but I'd say it's pretty shitty equally." Having lived his whole life in Kentucky, he felt that both towns he had lived in were extremely conservative, and the fact that they both overwhelmingly voted for Donald Trump in 2016 was a clear indication to him that he would not be accepted if people knew he was trans. Like Theo, Samuel had to drive out of town to get his testosterone. He drove 45 minutes to pick up his prescription because after he legally changed his name the pharmacist in his town said that they would no longer fill his testosterone prescription. Up until that point, the pharmacist hadn't realized he was trans and was fine filling the prescription. Samuel also had a lot of trouble finding a therapist and someone to perform his top surgery and hysterectomy in Kentucky: "You know, it doesn't matter how much money you fucking make or what kind of benefits you got, it fucking sucks being trans around here."

While this fear and understanding of living in the South and rural areas was very real to the trans men I spoke with, at the same time some described unexpected positive experiences. Later in my conversation with Mason he conveyed a couple stories to me about why he lived in rural areas and planned to keep it that way. I'll share one of those stories to demonstrate how even those men who most closely approached the hegemonic masculine standard in the region often surprised the trans men I spoke with by being completely welcoming. Mason was invited to Thanksgiving dinner with a friend who was in a same-sex, interracial relationship. She was black, and her girlfriend was white, and they had been invited to Thanksgiving dinner with the white woman's family "out in the hollers, this was out in the mountains . . . this was like fifty miles, sixty miles from town, and town is different than city, right? Town is just a town that might have a Walmart and a gas station." His friend told him, "You have to go with me man, I don't know if I'm gonna die." So, Mason joined them and "after a couple of mason jars of moonshine," he told the family he was trans and didn't know what to expect. He definitely didn't expect what happened next; they said, "Get out the Wild Turkey 101, we're gonna celebrate." He described the rest of the night as them "welcoming me into this man's world, this brother kind of world and . . . that always stuck with me."

THE DEMOGRAPHICS

The majority of the trans men I spoke with (30 of 51) identified their gender as male (all used the term "male," rather than "man"). These respondents preferred not to use the term "trans," largely due to the inappropriate questions and assumptions that followed. I will discuss this decision in more detail throughout the book. About a quarter (12 of 51) of respondents identified their gender as trans, including trans man, trans male, transgender, FTM (female-to-male), trans masculine, two-spirit, non-binary, genderqueer, or a combination of these identities. The remaining nine interviewees identified as both male and trans, depending on the circumstances. Most of these respondents usually identified only as male, but felt it was important to acknowledge their history or trans identity in some situations. I have changed all of the respondents' names for confidentiality purposes and I use the pronouns he, him, and his throughout the book because all respondents use these pronouns (some also use they, them, and theirs).

In terms of sexuality, the sample was diverse, with 18 of 51 trans men I spoke with identifying as heterosexual or straight. In total, 22 trans men identified as monosexual, four of whom identified as gay. Twenty-six respondents identified their sexuality as bi+, including bisexual, pansexual, queer, polysexual, demisexual, polysexual, fluid, or a combination thereof. Of the remaining three respondents, two identified as asexual and one did not identify with any sexuality label. Prior to transition, over half (29 of 51) of the interviewees identified as lesbian. This is consistent with prior research on trans men, and could be part of the reason trans men often face prejudice in the lesbian community, which I will explore more in Chapter 6. In addition to identifying as lesbian prior to transition, seven trans men identified as heterosexual or straight, four as gay, 10 as bi+, and one did not identify with any label. Thus, prior to identifying as trans, almost 80 percent (40 of 51) identified as monosexual, the majority of whom were only attracted to women.

While the trans men I spoke with were predominantly white (38 of 51), six identified their race as black or African American, two as Hispanic, four as multiracial or biracial, and one as Indigenous. While the goal of qualitative research is not generalization to an entire population, I was curious how closely the racial demographics of this group of men mirrored the demographics of the states in which they were located. Based on information from the 2018 population estimates at the United States Census Bureau, I averaged the percentage of white, black, Hispanic, and multiracial people from the eight Southeastern states represented by men in this study. These numbers closely resemble the group of trans men I spoke with. The eight Southern states averaged 74.1 percent white (compared to 75 percent of the respondents in this study), 20 percent black (compared to 12 percent in this study), 9.6 percent

Hispanic (compared to 4 percent in this study), 0.7 percent American Indian or Alaskan Native (compared to 0.2 percent in this study), and 2.2 percent two or more races (compared to 8 percent in this study). Therefore, while the percentages of black and Hispanic respondents were a little lower than the region average (largely due to the disproportionately high percentage of black people in Georgia and Hispanic people in Florida), the percentage of biracial or multiracial respondents was well above the regional average.

Finally, the average age of the sample was 29 years old, with ages ranging from 18 to 60. The younger respondents often attended college, or even high school, at a time when being trans was at least discussed, if not beginning to move towards acceptance. On the other hand, many of the older trans men I spoke with did not even hear the word "trans" until they were adults. These experiences clearly shaped their identities and their understandings of what it means to be trans. The group of trans men I spoke with also represented a diverse group of respondents in terms of socioeconomic class. Eleven respondents were working on or had completed a master's degree at the time of our interview. Additionally, eighteen of the trans men I talked to were working on or had completed a bachelor's degree and nine an associate's degree. Eleven respondents had completed some college, but had not completed a degree when we spoke, and the remaining two respondents had obtained their high school diplomas. Eleven of the 51 interviewees were full-time students or unemployed; the rest were working. While the vast majority of the respondents had at least some college, all but two respondents reported a yearly income of below $50,000 a year. Despite having higher than average educational credentials, most of the trans men I spoke with held working-class jobs and often struggled financially. A large portion of the respondents worked in retail jobs, and over half (29 of 51) made less than $25,000 a year. Table 0.1 provides demographic characteristics of the respondents.

ORGANIZATION OF THE BOOK

This book examines various aspects of trans men's experiences in the Southeast. As Sumerau and Mathers (2019, 12) explain, it is time that "we flip existing models of social science to present a portrait of the US society from the perspective of a marginalized community in hopes of facilitating greater understanding and integration of transgender perspectives more broadly." Therefore, I provide the story from the perspective of trans people, rather than from the perspective of cis people who hold power in our society. This allows respondents to continue the conversation about how trans people experience society, rather than being viewed through the lens of cis people. Lombardi

Table 0.1. Demographics

Name	Age	Years in South	Gender Identity	Sexual Identity	Race	Current State	Rural, Suburban, Urban	Education
Gordon	41	37	Male	Straight	White	GA	Rural	Associate's
Nolan	36	36	Male/Trans male	Straight	White	GA	Suburban	Master's
Kevin	34	34	Male	Pansexual	Multiracial	GA	Urban	Some College
Derek	34	34	Male	Gay	White	GA	Rural	Master's
Damien	38	34	Male	Pansexual	Multiracial	FL	Urban	Master's
Mason	34		Two-Spirit/Trans masculine	Queer/Fluid	Indigenous	TN	Rural	Some College
		30						
Liam	34	30	Male/FTM	Gay	White	TN	Urban	Bachelor's
Levi	45	30	Male	Pansexual	Black	TN	Suburban	Some College
Jeffrey	35	30	Male	Queer	White	VA	Rural	Bachelor's
Jayden	30	30	Trans man	Straight	White	VA	Urban	Associate's
Spencer	29		Male/FTM	Queer/ Pansexual	White	GA	Urban	Master's
		29						
Dakota	30	29	Male	Straight	White	SC	Urban	Some College
Stuart	28	28	Trans male/FTM	Straight	White	TN	Rural	Associate's
Jamar	30		Male	Demi/ Pansexual	White	TN	Suburban	Some College
		28						
Colton	28	28	Male/Trans man	Straight	White	SC	Suburban	Associate's
Gabriel	28	27	Male	Straight	Hispanic	SC	Suburban	Master's
Vincent	27	26	Male	Straight	White	PA	Urban	Bachelor's
Walker	51	25	Male	Bisexual	White	TN	Rural	Bachelor's
Trip	25	25	Transgender man	Queer	White	GA	Suburban	Master's
Javier	28	25	Male	Straight	Black	GA	Urban	Some College
Emmett	25	25	Male	Straight	White	AR	Rural	Associate's
Alec	25		Transgender male/ Genderqueer	Straight	White	TN	Urban	Some College
		25						
Theo	24	24	Male	Straight	White	SC	Rural	Master's
Jorge	24	23	Male	Pansexual	White	GA	Suburban	Some College
Bruno	23	23	Male	Polysexual	White	SC	Rural	High School

(continued)

Table 0.1. (continued)

Name	Age	Years in South	Gender Identity	Sexual Identity	Race	Current State	Rural, Suburban, Urban	Education
Samuel	22	22	Trans man	Queer	White	KY	Suburban	Bachelor's
Rowen	22	22	Male	Straight	White	GA	Suburban	High School
Hayden	32	22	Male	Pansexual	Multiracial	GA	Suburban	Associate's
Garrett	22	22	Male/Trans guy	Pansexual	White	GA	Suburban	Bachelor's
Darius	23	22	Male	Asexual	White	GA	Urban	Some College
Timothy	21	21	Male	Bisexual	White	SC	Suburban	Associate's
Sage	23	21	Trans man	Queer	White	NY	Urban	Master's
Maddox	21	21	Male	Bisexual	White	GA	Rural	Bachelor's
Hugh	25	21	Male	No Label	White	GA	Suburban	Bachelor's
Billy	22	21	Male	Queer	White	GA	Urban	Some College
Zac	20	20	Male/FTM	Bisexual	White	GA	Urban	Bachelor's
Tobias	19	19	Male	Pansexual	White	GA	Rural	Bachelor's
Reece	18	18	Male	Pansexual	Multiracial	GA	Rural	Bachelor's
Jace	18	18	Male	Bisexual	White	GA	Suburban	Associate's
Donnie	28	17	Male/Trans male	Bi/Pansexual	White	VA	Suburban	Bachelor's
Leo	30	15	Male	Straight	Black	NC	Suburban	Master's
Frank	41	15	Male	Straight	White	SC	Urban	Bachelor's
Carter	26	12	Transgender	Bi/Pansexual	White	TN	Urban	Bachelor's
Andre	33	11	Male/Trans male	Straight	Black	GA	Urban	Associate's
Quentin	34	10	Male	Straight	Black	GA	Rural	Some College
Jamie	33	7	Trans man	Gay	White	AR	Urban	Bachelor's
Ronald	60	6	Male/Trans man	Straight	Black	GA	Urban	Bachelor's
Max	18	4	Male	Bi/Pansexual	Hispanic	GA	Rural	Bachelor's
Dayton	36	4	Trans masculine/ Non-binary	Pansexual	White	FL	Suburban	Master's
Parker	23	2	Trans masculine	Asexual	White	VA	Urban	Master's
Eli	19	1	Transgender	Gay	White	SC	Urban	Bachelor's

(2018, 68–70) explains, "Social research is dominated by cis narratives of trans people and trans lives. . . . The dominance of cis voices in explaining the trans experience continues to limit what we know about trans lives." I add to Sumerau and Mathers' project by focusing on how geographic location influences experiences and continue Abelson's (2019) call to move trans studies forward by taking seriously the claim that place matters. Additionally, this book focuses solely on the Southeast, where queer people are overrepresented in terms of numbers, but largely underrepresented in terms of social scientific research (Stone 2018).

In Chapter 1, Becoming Trans, I explore what it means to be trans and three common experiences trans men in the South navigate in becoming trans. These three experiences include coming out as trans, choosing and legally changing your name, and physical transitions. In the section on coming out, I focus on trans men's experience of realizing they were trans and coming out to themselves. While a lot of research considers the experience of coming out to others, especially in regard to minority sexualities, less research has examined the importance of coming out to one's self. The next two sections of Chapter 1 look at how trans men in the South choose their names, how and whether they legally change their names, and how and whether they choose to physically transition their bodies.

Chapter 2, Trans Manhood, explores the meaning of manhood to trans men in the South. Additionally, in this chapter I assess how trans men's understanding of manhood and masculinity aligns with how they do gender and do masculinities. I also explore whether trans men's versions of masculinities are better, or more healthy, than cis men's. Then, I ask whether gender equality will ever be reached if we continue to define manhood the way we do and if men continue to feel pressure to do masculinity in ways that demonstrate their dominance over others.

Various normativities in our society have begun to gain attention in the media and in social science research. In Chapter 3, Born in the Wrong Body, I explore the impacts of transnormativity on the lives of trans men in the South. I look at the narratives trans men tell about their gender identity, specifically the "born in the wrong body" and "discovery" narratives, and question the impacts of these narratives. Despite the continued use of these narratives, often due to medical gatekeepers, this chapter ends on a hopeful note that transnormativity within the trans community may be on the decline. That is, most of the men I spoke to did not feel that biomedical interventions were necessary for someone to "really" be trans.

In Chapter 4, Passing in the South, I assess the importance of "passing," or being recognized as men. I point to three main reasons why trans men in the South desire to pass, and often conceal their trans identities. These reasons include self-confidence and psychological health, the privileges of being a cisgender man, and safety and fear of violence. I explore each of these reasons and demonstrate why these are pronounced in the Southeast.

Chapter 5, Losing My Religion, provides an exploratory look at trans men and religion in the South. I show the continued importance of religion in the region, look at how trans men negotiate their trans identities with their religious and/or spiritual beliefs, and question what influence these negotiations will have on the oppression of trans men. While research has begun to look at how cisgender Christians view trans people, little has examined how trans people view religion and spirituality and if they are able to overcome the potential cognitive dissonance between the two identities of trans and religious, specifically Christian.

Much of this book focuses on the prejudice, discrimination, and oppression trans people face in our broader society, but Chapter 6, Discord Within the Queer Community, specifically examines these negative experiences within the queer community. In this chapter, I explore how trans men navigate the queer community and whether they feel accepted or rejected by this community based on their trans identities. I show that trans men experience numerous incidents of prejudice and discrimination from cis gay men, cis lesbian women, and other trans people. I also provide a glimpse into how these experiences vary based on the men's other intersecting characteristics, including sexuality, race, and class.

Chapter 7, Sexual Harassment and Assault, provides an overview of trans men's experiences with sexual violence in the South. In this chapter, I discuss how trans men's experiences of sexual violence differ before and after transition. The stories of the men in this study show that being recognized as a woman in our society dramatically increases the chances of sexual victimization. After being recognized as men, sexual victimization occurred much less frequently, and usually with the intention of proving to the men that they were not men. This chapter adds to the growing literature on sexual victimization by including a population that is often overlooked in this literature.

I conclude the book with suggestions for moving forward and improving the lives of trans men in the Southeast. I also include an appendix on the methodology I used in this study, with a call for continuing to queer sociological methods.

NOTE

1. All interviewees have been anonymized through the use of pseudonyms.

Chapter One

Becoming Trans

Becoming—a verb meaning to undergo change or development (Merriam-Webster Dictionary 2019). Becoming is a process. Becoming is a career. Becoming trans acknowledges the process of development trans people go through to find themselves, or for the world to see them as they see themselves. Some may argue that "becoming trans" is inappropriate, that "being trans" is more accurate; however, being trans ignores the process. This is why Garner (2014, 30) argues, "*Becoming* is a highly productive concept in transgender studies and in theoretical perspectives on the body in general because of its capacity to provide a way of reconsidering the nature of the body and body modification. In particular, it has the potential to undermine the accusation that trans bodies are unnatural or constructed." Becoming takes seriously the reality of gender as a continuous doing by all people (West and Zimmerman 2009).

Becoming also acknowledges that the "coming out" process is never complete. While this process varies, and is unique for each individual, there are some common experiences most trans people must navigate. In fact, some scholars, such as Guittar (2014), believe the concept of process doesn't go far enough in describing coming out; that it doesn't capture the true nature of gender and sexual identity development. Speaking specifically of coming out as a sexual minority, Guittar (2014, 125, emphasis in original) argues that "*coming out as a gradual process* and *coming out as a career* are similar in that they both recognize coming out as an ongoing progression. However, there is a sharp distinction between these two conceptions of coming out: a process is eventually completed, while a career is not completed, per se—it is merely managed." Whether the language of becoming, process, or career can fully capture what is taking place or not, they are all used to demonstrate that holding a marginal identity requires a lifetime of transformation and development. One is never fully out, or never arrives at an identity completely. Rather we must all manage our identities on an endless basis.

In our society, cisnormative and heteronormative assumptions force queer people to constantly struggle for self-affirmation and acceptance by others. Queer people are rarely allowed to just *be*. We are not "born this way," although this is a narrative commonly used to describe queer identities (and I will discuss this narrative more in Chapter 3), but must perpetually become ourselves. The trans men I spoke with talked about how their gender and sexual identities shifted multiple times throughout their lives. Some thought they were gender non-binary, then realized they actually felt more comfortable identifying as men. Some discussed how their sexuality changed after their gender changed. Some discussed how no matter how much your body changes, you will always be trans, because you do not have the socialization of cis men. For instance, Bruno put it this way: "The bottom line is you're still trans, no matter what you do to yourself . . . you're not magically gonna become cis just because you had a surgical procedure." Either way, whether they put it into these words or not, each respondent discussed being trans as a process of finding themselves, and for most a process that was ongoing.

In this chapter, I examine three common experiences most of the respondents dealt with in becoming trans. These common processes are meant to describe a typical experience of becoming trans in the Southeast; they are in no way prescriptive, meaning they are not what trans men *should* do, but rather are descriptive of what the men in this study told me they *do*. Also, this does not mean these experiences will occur, or if they do, that they will be similar to other trans men in the South. Psychological stage models, such as Coleman's (1981) developmental stages of the coming out process, propose a linear progression of developmental process, and were a helpful starting place for understanding gender and sexual development. However, research has shown that these models are much more complicated than first described (Guittar 2014). For more information and an identity development model for trans people, see Beemyn and Rankin's (2011) book, *The Lives of Transgender People.*

The three common experiences I discuss in this chapter are: 1) "coming out" as trans to one's self; 2) choosing and legally changing your name; and 3) physically transitioning one's body to align with one's gender identity, usually through hormones and/or gender affirmation surgeries (historically referred to as sex reassignment surgery). In many cases, these three experiences happened sequentially in this order. In others they happened in a different order or simultaneously, and in others one or more of these experiences did not occur or have yet to occur. Each trans person has a unique story of becoming trans and each person's story continued after this brief moment we spoke in 2018. Here I provide a glimpse into some of the commonalities and narratives the respondents used to describe what this process looked like for them.

COMING OUT

What is "coming out" and is it still relevant in society today? Guittar (2014) explores these questions in-depth regarding sexuality. While "coming out" as trans differs from coming out as lesbian, bisexual, gay, etc., there are similarities among these experiences. These similarities are largely due to the structural nature of the coming out process. As Guittar explains, "In order to understand the continued relevance of coming out and its role in contemporary society, we must consider the following fact: *coming out is a function of oppression.* Those groups which enjoy positions of privilege in society rarely, if ever, have to analyze, question, disclose, or justify the characteristics of their dominant traits" (4). Therefore, while the specifics may vary, the commonalities that arise from revealing a marginalized identity to self and to others demonstrate the continued importance of the concept of "coming out" for all queer people today.

While much of the research on coming out focuses on the process of telling others about one's sexuality, a key aspect of coming out involves acknowledging this identity to one's self. It is an acknowledgment that your sexuality, or gender identity in this case, differs from what others expect based on the sex you were assigned at birth and the cis- and heteronormative assumptions that follow that assignment. As Guittar (2014, 27) shows, "self-acceptance is quite central to coming out and not merely a prerequisite." In fact, some of Guittar's respondents used the terms "self-acceptance" and "coming out" synonymously.

In a study of trans college students, Nicolazzo (2017, 1), who also identifies as trans, found that coming out was a moment that all of their participants were able to pinpoint, or at least "able to tap into a general feeling or sentiment when we noticed for the first time that we were different, that we were not like the other people with who we shared" our lives. Together, these moments of coming out as trans serve two purposes:

> First, they set up a world in which we recognize our difference. In these moments, through these feelings and in recovering these stories, we uncover how our trans* becomings—or the ways we are always already coming into our unfolding trans*ness (Garner 2014)—cast us outside and other than the perceived norm of gendered living. Although many of us . . . lack the words in the moment to name this phenomenon, this is the first time we bump up against transgender oppression, or the systemic presumption that there are two immutable, fixed genders (i.e., man and woman) that frames those of us who do not fit this norm as abnormal, abject, wrong, or otherwise less than our cisgender peers. . . . The

second way these stories operate is to bring forward a new "us" into which "we" enter. In effect, our coming out as trans* acts as a *coming in* of sorts. (1)

By this Nicolazzo is referring to a coming into community with other trans people. In this section, I examine how the trans men I spoke with *become* trans, acknowledge this becoming to themselves, and come into acceptance and community through this emerging identity.

Coming Out to One's Self

The process of trans people uncovering "our trans* becomings" (Nicolazzo 2017, 1) is a lifelong career. Coming out to self often takes years, or decades, after which we recognize we are becoming something new. Most of the men spoke of always knowing there was something different about themselves, but not being able to put a finger on it for a long time. Looking back, the men noticed many times when their gender did not fit in the established binary system. For these men, these stories become part of their discovery narratives, which I will discuss in more detail in Chapter 3. For now, I want to share some of these men's stories of coming out to themselves, or finally finding a label they felt fit their identity and made them feel part of a larger community.

Like many of the experiences in this book, age played a huge role in trans men's coming out processes. Previous research notes the generational differences in trans people's experiences (Beemyn and Rankin 2011; Sumerau and Mathers 2019), and nowhere is this difference more pronounced than in their understandings of their own identities and coming out, or coming to terms with their identity as trans. As Sumerau and Mathers (2019) note, trans people who choose not to come out to others, or have a harder time accepting their own trans identity, are often over 30 years old. A lot of this has to do with the limited information that was available when older trans people started to realize they were different from what others expected them to be (Beemyn and Rankin 2011).

Many of the trans men I spoke with discussed not knowing what trans meant when they started to realize they were different and not having any role models in the trans community to help them understand their identity. Mason, who was 34 years old when we spoke, said:

I've always thought that I was a boy, until that wonderful time in a person's life where they learn that that's not how their body is equipped. I always knew that I didn't identify with the body that I was born into, but in the '80s and '90s we didn't have any trans visibility, so I didn't know what that was. So, you know, we latch onto the first label we configure. And, and I knew that I liked women, so I guess I would identify as a butch lesbian because that's the only thing that we had. Some folks would say, you know, tomboy or whatever labels that we had during the time period, but I never really identified with any of them until I learned about trans identities in late '90s, early 2000s. And so that's when [I knew I was trans].

Since trans people did not begin to gain media attention until the early 2000s, many of the trans men over 30 years old felt lost when trying to explain what was going on with their gender identities. This delayed the coming out process for many of the men I talked to, because they were not sure how to come out when they did not understand what was happening. This was also why many of the men spoke about coming out as butch lesbian women long before realizing what trans meant. Similar to Mason, Nolan, who was 36 years old when we spoke, said:

If I had to pinpoint a time where I solidified the concepts of transgender in mind and knew what that meant for me, I would have to say it was at the age of 14, when I first discovered the term transgender, and first started researching gender identity disorder, gender dysphoria, whatever you want to call it, it's changed names over the years. . . . That's when it became clear to me what all of these feelings I had been previously dealing with, it actually put . . . a label on it, a definition that it wasn't just something in my head.

In addition to trans visibility in the media, the advent of the Internet and easy access to information was another reason age played such a huge role in trans men's coming out stories. For Derek, as a teenager he realized his gender was different, but was even more confused because he was also attracted to men. He said:

I didn't see that anywhere else. There were no resources at the time. I'm 34 so this is the '90s. I was stuck doing it on my own. I started to see a therapist, more for the normal teenage adjustment stuff, but I eventually brought up that I didn't feel like a girl. I knew the word transsexual, but all I knew was that some men were born feeling like women. I tried to explain it to my therapist, but she was like, "No, that's not you. You're normal." I think she was trying to ease my mind, assuming I felt like something was wrong with me. So, she discouraged me from thinking that I was not a girl. Then, when I was in high school, I saw *Boys Don't Cry*. I don't remember what year it was exactly, but I remember it was the first time I saw someone like me. I had very mixed reactions to the movie. I was able to see someone like me, but at the same time it was shown as really bad. The person was beat, raped, and eventually killed. It was very traumatizing for me. Also, a lot of people conflated the movie with lesbianism. They assumed that he was a lesbian and that made me confused, because I was never attracted to girls, so I just never fit in. . . . Well, I started feeling that way in high school. I tried to cut my hair and talked to some close friends about it.

I tried to move in that direction, but I was discouraged. Eventually, I gave up. I moved in the direction and wanted to identify as male, but never got there. So, I went back to identifying as a woman. I didn't begin identifying as trans until after college when I was around 23 years old. By that time, the Internet was way more accessible in 2007 so I could look things up.

Younger trans men have spent their entire lives with any information they need at their fingertips. For queer people over the age of 30, we often felt weird or different with no idea how to explain these feelings or find labels and definitions for what was going on so that, like Nolan commented, we could rest assured this "wasn't just something in [our] head."

Levi, a 45-year-old black pansexual male from Tennessee, explained, for many of these men, lesbian was the only label they could find any information about at the time, although even that information was often limited, stereotypical, and derogatory, but at least it meant they weren't alone. Levi said:

> I did identify as a lesbian for a long time, but it was because I honestly didn't really know of transgenderism, I didn't really know anything but gay and lesbian. . . . When I discovered [the lesbian] community I thought I'd just automatically fit into the lesbian category, because obviously, I like women, so, that's what I identified with. I've always been very much a tomboy. . . . I've not really ever liked like feminine pronouns or anything, they've always . . . annoyed me and even, that was even before I really understood, you know, what transgender was, or that it was something. So, it was always something, that kind of unsettling. . . . During that period, it was always just something within me that I wasn't happy with, you know? And I didn't really know how to label it or what to call it, or why I was, because, I mean, I had a good life, you know? And I started researching, I just started going on the Internet and kind of researching, just typing in my feelings and how I felt and that's how the discovery began as far as what I actually was. . . . I started researching this in my late 20s, I would say around 28.

Again, they felt something was not exactly right, but had no words to describe it. These men felt lost and confused, and no one in their networks were able to help them. Ronald, a 60-year-old black straight trans man, did not learn that trans men existed until he saw Chaz Bono on TV in 2012. Chaz Bono, son of Sonny Bono and Cher, came out nationally as a trans man in 2009 and was the subject of a documentary, *Becoming Chaz*, in 2011. Ronald said:

> I was like wow I didn't know this was a thing, this explains everything. I didn't accept it right away, but that's when I started thinking it. It took me about 3 years to finally tell someone, other than my therapist. When I told a close friend, and she didn't freak out I was like maybe I can do this. I was scared to tell people because people did not react well when I came out as lesbian. I was in the Bay area and I got beat up when I came out. So, finally after I accepted it

I started HRT [hormone replacement therapy] in October 2015. But, even after that it took me 3 to 4 years to begin to "embrace my maleness." I held on to the lesbian label until February of 2016. After the hormones started working and I legally changed my name, that's when I came out to everyone.

When I asked Dayton, a 36-year-old white pansexual non-binary trans masculine person, to discuss when he knew he was trans, he said:

That's kind of tough to answer, because I didn't have any vocabulary to think of myself, so, I knew I felt different and thought maybe I was an alien or something, 'cause I didn't, I only heard about, I only heard the term transgender, when I had a client who was transgender and transitioning, and that was . . . like two years ago. . . . When I was little, I felt really bummed that I was, I had to be a girl, you know, or so I thought, so . . . I just kind of, you know, accepted it and . . . experienced lots of depression.

While labels can obviously be problematic and limiting for some people, they can also be empowering and freeing. Without a vocabulary of what it meant to be trans, many of the men felt lost, depressed, and like they were "an alien" in their worlds.

For younger trans men, like Jace, an 18-year-old white bisexual male, the information they needed to understand their own identities and come out to themselves as trans was located much quicker, and usually at a much younger age. Jace realized he felt different when he was 16, and by the time we spoke less than two years later he had figured out his identity as trans and come out to himself. Here is his story:

I was sixteen and I had started being really depressed because, you know, I really didn't like being a lesbian, I didn't like the terminology for being a lesbian, and I was just really feeling socially awkward in my own skin. . . . I didn't like having a chest, I didn't like having long hair and I just felt like every time I looked in the mirror I felt like I shouldn't have had this be on my body, I felt like I shouldn't have everything that I have right now and I just kinda felt like I had been cheated or wronged. . . . I started talking to a really close friend of mine and he would tell me like, well why don't you, have you like looked at other options if you're really feeling this way? And he's like, "Because, like, right now, it sounds like you're trans." And I was like, well I don't even know what that is, how do I know that it's not just me being like socially awkward and just not liking my body, and he went on to tell me what trans is and how, and then we went on to look at some trans blogs and all that stuff and the more that I looked at trans guys, and looked at trans blogs, the more I realized that this is something that I would think I really fit into the category of, and, you know, I could see that happening to me, like seeing top surgery happening, seeing testosterone, and seeing myself become more masculine and it made sense.

And so, we just started simple with pronouns and then once a few months hit we started me talking about wanting to cut my hair and that felt like a big relief, and then I started to, like, slightly change the way I dressed and the more and more stuff I did, just basic simple stuff, the better my confidence was, the better my depression got and like it's not 100% fixed or anything, but it definitely is a lot better than where I was when I was 16.

While younger trans men still struggled with their identities and coming out, they had a lot more room for experimentation and a lot more information available. A friend suggesting that you might be trans was something that none of the older respondents experienced. The older respondents were much more likely to experience people telling them they were not trans, or it was just a phase.

Like Jace, another young respondent, Maddox, who was 21 years old, quickly came to terms with his trans identity. Maddox explained, "I didn't even know what the word transgender meant until I was about 17 years old, and then . . . when I learned what it was, I was like, 'Oh, that's me, that's what I feel.'" Many of the younger men made it seem like an easy process to come out to oneself; they learned what trans meant, researched it, and then almost immediately accepted the label. For instance, Samuel, who was 22 years old, said (emphasis mine):

I always like pretended to be a boy online as I was growing up . . . but I just had no idea that being trans existed . . . I grew up in a small Kentucky town . . . I didn't even know any gay people and so *I figured out I was trans kind of the moment I realized that it was a thing.* . . . I had an idea of trans women, of course not positive ones, just from watching like Jerry Springer and Maury with dad, but I had no idea that trans men existed and I remember . . . I watched like every queer thing that Netflix had from the moment we got Netflix on like, all through when I was growing up so I was like, I don't know, I was in middle school so I'd watch like every gay thing they had on Netflix and I would literally just pore over every single, if it was a LGBT title section, I watched it and I think somewhere in doing that it led me onto YouTube and somehow I saw . . . a video . . . and it was like as soon as I saw it, I was like, "Oh shit, that's it, that's what it is." . . . As soon as I knew it was a thing I knew that's what it was and I'd had like tons of mental health issues up to that point and it just kind of all made sense after that. . . . I was really young.

Finally, when I asked Theo, who was 24 years old, how he knew he was trans, he said, "I don't know, I guess I was just searching it . . . on the internet, reading stories, and then . . . *one day it just kind of clicked*, I was like, this isn't right. I wasn't supposed to be this butch lesbian that I was, and I was always more comfortable in male's clothes and male names, and

I was like I think this is where I wanna go, and I haven't had any problems with it yet" (emphasis mine). This is not to say younger trans men have not struggled or faced prejudice, discrimination, or oppression based on being trans. Yet coming to terms with the identity of being trans appears to have gotten much easier in the last decade. For most of the younger respondents, coming out as trans to one's self was something that just "clicked." The increased visibility of trans people, and the increased acceptance of difference among younger generations, has made a positive difference in the experience of coming out as trans in the Southeast.

WHAT'S IN A NAME?

Naming is another important part of becoming trans for many people. As Ray (2015) discusses in his autobiography, "I realize that knowing my own name has carried the most weight in my life story. Until I knew my own name, I was completely unable to name the big truths—good and bad—about myself; I was unable to be honest with myself. I couldn't name my passions, the parts of myself that I loved, or the parts of myself that I wished weren't real until I truly knew how to name myself." As this quote demonstrates, it is difficult, or impossible, to know yourself and your dreams without first knowing your own name. In a study of trans kids, Travers (2018) argues, "Being called a 'boy' or a 'girl' and assigned correspondingly gendered names and pronouns are two of the dimensions of power that adults exercise over children and that shape how they experience their world." Almost all (47 of 51) of the respondents in this study went by a different name than they were assigned at birth and all went by different pronouns. Changing their name(s) and pronouns allowed them to take some of that power back and to shape their own worlds. Accordingly, most respondents legally changed their name(s) (28 of 51) or planned to in the future (18 of 51).

Each of the men told me a unique story of how they chose their name and the process of legally changing their name(s). Often in the trans community, the name a person was assigned at birth is referred to as their "dead name." Someone calling a trans person by the name they were assigned at birth is called "dead naming." This is a major problem within the trans community. Dead naming is used both intentionally—as a form of discrimination and oppression—and unintentionally—by those who know a person is trans and forget to use their chosen name. Hence, dead naming is a form of both overt discrimination and a microaggression—a subtle slight—used to demonstrate that a person is not fully accepted into society. While all of the respondents chose to go by gender binary pronouns—he, him, his (although some also used they, them, theirs, depending on the situation)—the majority felt very strongly about the importance of picking the correct name.

Choosing Your Name

One common theme that arose in how respondents chose their names was their relationships with their families, and specifically their parents. Especially for those with supportive families, honoring their parents was an important component of picking a name. Some of the men's parents told them the name they had picked out for them if they had been born a boy and these respondents chose this as their first or middle name to honor their parents' and their ability to choose the name of their children. Others chose to use, or modify, nicknames their family had given them growing up, or use a more masculine or modified version of their dead name. Some chose names that sounded similar to their names assigned at birth or that had the same initials in order to make the transition easier for those around them.

Spencer, a 29-year-old white queer FTM, choose his name for a variety of these reasons, including that "it's the closest to my birth name and I wanted to kind of keep it similar . . . to pay respect to my parents and the choices they made, but also be what I choose. . . . I would equate it to the masculine form of what my birth name is . . . pretty much the exact name, just masculine." Similarly, Bruno wanted to honor his grandma who he was originally named after so he legally changed his middle name to be her surname because it was not feminine, but demonstrated his respect for her.

Another interviewee, Sage, a 23-year-old white queer trans man, planned to change his name legally, but hadn't yet because of his family. Even though he was in graduate school and no longer financially dependent on his family, he didn't want to do anything that would jeopardize their relationship. His family was "very attached" to his name and "they get very defensive and upset when it comes to talking about legally changing things." While his mom was working hard to be sure to call him by his chosen name, he still felt he needed to legally change his name to be able to move forward. Sage said the subject was something he plans to "broach again," but he was treading lightly because he didn't want to upset the delicate balance they had established. He was enjoying the closeness of their relationship and felt it was necessary to discuss the issue with them again before starting the name change process. The importance of family and relationships were clear in these discussions; respondents did not want their decision to change their name to have a negative influence on those who had supported them to that point.

On the other hand, some respondents specifically changed their name(s) due to their strained and toxic relationships with their parents. For instance,

Jorge, a 24-year-old white pansexual male who lived in Georgia, explained he changed his last name, because "at the time, my parents were not supportive and so I just wanted to cut all ties and that was my big final, 'FU, I'm done with you.'" Last names in patriarchal cultures are usually passed down from the father and originally this was a sign of the father's ownership of his wife and children. Today, in the United States most heterosexual families continue to be recognized under the name of the father. While most people no longer view this as a sign of property ownership, it is still used as a sign of unity and family cohesiveness. Therefore, choosing to change your last name, outside of a woman marrying a man, is symbolic of breaking ties with your family. By choosing a different last name, some trans men meant to sever unhealthy relationships with their families of origin and start fresh, as themselves.

Emmett, a 25-year-old white straight male in rural Arkansas, explained, "I actually got my last name from my stepfather that accepts me, because my biological father wants nothing to do with me." He used taking his step-father's last name as a sign of respect and gratitude for his acceptance that stood in stark contrast to his biological father who did not accept him for who he was. Emmett also shared a middle name with his mother prior to transition; when he changed his middle name to a more masculine version of the name, she did also so they would still have the same middle name. This level of support is very encouraging and uplifting, especially in the rural South. A couple other respondents also chose to change their last name to their mother's maiden name, instead of keeping their father's last name. Overall, there was more support from mothers than from fathers when it came to gender transition.

While most of the men's choices of names had something to do with their history (for instance, choosing a name based on ethnic heritage to keep a connection with their roots) or family, there were other methods of choosing a name discussed in the interviews. Some men chose their name through drag kinging. This made sense because they had learned about masculinities and being a man through drag; therefore, using that name helped them remember where they started. Also, people were used to calling them by their drag name from their time performing so this made the transition to their new name easier, especially in the queer community. Only a few respondents indicated they chose their names from a list of masculine names with no particular type of attachment to the name they picked.

Out of the 51 trans men I talked to, only four chose not to change their names legally. They made this decision because they held a sentimental attachment to their name, their name was gender neutral enough to suit them, or it just "didn't bother them." Nolan had a sentimental attachment to his name: "My grandmother named me and I'm proud of it, so I have no interest in changing my name." Only one respondent said he was not sure if he would eventually change his name.

Legally Changing Your Name

However respondents chose their names, many faced pushback and compli-cations when they tried to legally change their name. Each state has different laws for the process of legally changing your name (as well as legally chang-ing your gender marker on various forms of identification). These processes and laws are extremely important because without the right to change this information, your dead name and the sex you were assigned at birth can haunt you for the rest of your life. As Alec, a 25-year-old white straight transgender male who had lived his whole life in the South, explained, "Because I was born in Tennessee . . . I will never be able to change my gender marker on my birth certificate. I can change my name on it, but I can't change my gender marker. At the end of the day, that freaking piece of paper is gonna haunt me for the rest of my life."

Because each state has different laws, here I am going to use the process in Georgia for illustration; a process Maddox described as "long, tedious, and expensive." To legally change your name in Georgia, you must complete the following steps (this information can be found at the National Center for Trans-gender Equality ID Documents Center; here you can also find details about the specific requirements for name changes in any state). First, you have to submit a petition to the court and pay $209; this includes five forms that must be filled out and taken to the Clerk of Court for the Superior Court at your county's courthouse. You can apply to have the fee waived by demonstrating "indigence" (extreme poverty that would be effected by paying the $209 fee). Within seven days of filing this petition, you must publish a notice of the name change in the county's "official legal organ," once a week for four weeks. This means, you must pay to have your name change request published in the county's newspaper for four weeks in order to give people in the county time and the right to object to your name change. This process usually costs between $30 and $100, depending on where you live and the newspaper's fees. After the official waiting period of 30 days, and the publication notice for four weeks, you must schedule your final hearing with a judge and appear before them. Ul-timately, your name change is dependent on the judge you are assigned in your county approving the name change and signing off on a final order.

As should be clear from this description, legally changing your name can be a long, intimidating, and expensive process. Many conservative states have placed increased regulations and restrictions on this process that lead to unfair burdens on trans people in these states. Trans men in Georgia specifically discussed three major problems with this process: cost, appearing before a judge, and publishing the name change publicly in a newspaper. Spencer explained how the cost and the amount of time it took made the entire process challenging:

> It was frustrating and expensive. . . . I had to go to the courthouse and pretty much file it and it was like $250, and then I had to go to the newspaper and put an ad for four weeks, which is like $100, and then wait forever. . . . I started the process at the end of May, and I waited . . . until June, and then nobody said anything [regarding the post in the newspaper], so it went to the court, but I didn't have a court date until September.

The process is unnecessarily expensive, intimidating, and drawn out. When a cis woman marries a cis man, if she chooses to change her last name there is no additional paperwork required, other than changing her identifications. However, in some states, if that same cis woman wants to change her name back to her maiden name after a divorce, she has to follow the same steps as trans men in Georgia: paying, putting it in the newspaper, and going before a judge. Obviously, this process is set up to privilege cis heterosexual men, who never have to change their names based on the outdated traditions in this country.

Trip, a 25-year-old white queer transgender man who had lived his entire life in Georgia, explained how the court gave him a hard time when he tried to change his name legally before he went on hormones and had his top surgery. After he started physically transitioning, they allowed him to change his name, but seemed less than enthusiastic about it. When he appeared in front of the judge for him to rule on the name change, Trip said, the judge

> had a name change right before me and he seemed really kind of excited to change this girl's name, she had just gotten married. And then when it came to mine he kind of was very legal about it, just like, 'Are you frauding anybody?' No. 'Are you gonna do this?' Yes. 'Then your name is changed. Pick up the paperwork later' and that was it.

If the process was not already intimidating enough, having to stand before a noticeably transphobic judge to have your fate determined is cruel and unusual punishment. Other respondents had judges tell them they could not change their names or shame them in open court. Had Trip not looked like what the judge expected of a man, this process would have been even more traumatic.

The name change process in Georgia is so stressful that one of the men I spoke with moved to another state for the sole purpose of changing his name. Liam, a 34-year-old white gay FTM person, described it this way:

> I actually moved out of state so I could [change my name]. . . . In Georgia they publish, it right? So, it may be published for like a couple of months in a legal

paper, but we can just like Google that shit. . . . I knew that whoever looked up my new name was gonna get that for results. That includes, like jobs and shit. . . . So, in order to avoid the situation where the bosses . . . see I used to be [my name assigned at birth] or whoever the hell else. We really shouldn't be seeing that shit. I went up to Tennessee and I actually got like a whole different job there and a different address [so I could change my name there].

This is why many of the respondents who wanted to legally change their name had not yet. All but two of the men I spoke with made less than $50,000 a year, and the majority (29 of 51) made less than $25,000. Paying to legally change their names was a huge burden, so moving to another state to do this was totally out of the question. Nonetheless, as Liam explained, to have your name change published in a newspaper in the digital age meant that this would follow you for the rest of your life. In a country where there are no legal protections for trans people in terms of being fired from a job, evicted from your home, etc., this move cost Liam a lot of money, but in his calculations it was well worth the hardship in order to protect him in the future.

Assuming you have $239 to $309, you have the ability to complete all of the forms and deliver them to the county courthouse, you are able to publish the name change in the newspaper without the threat of violence or fear of future retribution, and you get a trans-friendly judge who approves your name change, then you have completed step one of legally changing your name. Within 60 days of legally changing your name, you are required to change your driver's license or state identification card to match your new name. To do this, you must present the legal name change documents to the Department of Motor Vehicles and may be required to pay renewal fees, depending on your license expiration date. Remember, this is just changing your name; to also change your gender marker on your Georgia identification, you must submit a separate court order or a physician's letter certifying gender change—meaning the date of your gender reassignment operation—as well as pay $5 for a gender change. Finally, if you wish to amend your gender marker on your birth certificate in the state of Georgia, the state requires "a certified copy of a court order indicating the sex of an individual born in this state has been changed by surgical procedure and that individual's name has been changed." This is a separate court order from the name change; it will require more money for another court order, fees to pay a physician for a medical appointment and to sign a medical certification, funds to have gender affirmation surgeries that align with the Georgia Code, and finally fees to process the new birth certificate. If all of this is not overwhelming enough, you also have to work with the federal government to change your passport and Social Security card, which also costs money, includes more forms, and more waiting.

Other states in the Southeast are not much better than Georgia. As Levi put it, "I'm actually in the process [of changing my name] . . . but it's a monetary thing. Every time I get ready to go pay the money, then life happens." Since changing your name costs so much, some respondents also explained that legally changing their names was less important than spending their money on their physical transitions, especially testosterone and top surgery. Bruno had chosen a new name and went by it, but said he hadn't legally changed it because "my name is actually less important to me . . . there are other things I'd rather do with the money, transition wise . . . save up for hormones . . . or put it towards top surgery, my name is like very much an afterthought for me." In fact, of the 18 trans men who planned to change their names legally in the future, 11 specifically mentioned money as a barrier to this process and for most of them the main reason they had not completed the process already.

For some respondents, there were other barriers, in addition to money. Gabriel, a 28-year-old Hispanic straight male, explained the stress of changing your name in South Carolina, where he went through the process:

> Oh god, that took forever. It was kind of a pain, cause like each county doesn't have the paperwork already drawn up, so I was able to find the information online, but then I had to do like a background check. . . . I had to write up the paperwork myself, and then I had to file the claim. . . . Because I had multiple name changes in the past, just because I had gotten married and then got divorced, the judge requested a court date. So, I had to go in and just kind of explain to her why I was requesting the name change and she said she didn't have any problems with it. . . . So, she granted it. . . . I think it ended up being close to like $200 by the time it was all said and done. Cause I had to get like fingerprints . . . the background check cost . . . then the court costs.

As I listened to his story, I expected this must have taken place a long time ago, but he said this was in 2015. Only a few years ago, a major county in South Carolina did not even have official paperwork to complete and each trans person seeking a name change was forced to figure out the entire process from scratch. Colton agreed with Gabriel that changing your name in South Carolina "[f]ucking sucked." He described it as a long drawn out process that costs "probably around $300," yet "you have to do it all within 90 days or else your fingerprints . . . will expire and you will have to get re-fingerprinted." The fingerprinting and background checks in South Carolina are just another example of the hurdles trans people have to navigate in the South, and conservative states more generally. The one good thing in South Carolina, compared to Georgia, was that you do not have to publish your name change in a newspaper that would continue to be public record for the rest of your life.

A few years earlier, in 2013, Samuel had a difficult time legally changing his name in Kentucky. Here is his story:

> [The name change process] was a fucking nightmare. I live in Kentucky and I'm from a small town in Kentucky. . . . I petitioned to change my name almost immediately after I turned 18 and the judge, I had to show up for court and stuff, which you know is intimidating enough, and then I get there . . . I'm standing in front of the fucking judge, and she tells me she has to think about it . . . I know that's illegal. It's nothing that she's got to think about . . . so she ended up changing it, presumably it just took however long for her to realize it was illegal for her to tell me no, and then she approved it, but they just mailed it to me and because of that being postponed like that I had to enroll in college under the wrong name. . . . It was just this continual ordeal like until I transferred [schools].

This brings up the issue of local policies, such as whether schools and employers allow you to go by your chosen name, or force you to go by your dead name. Many schools and workplaces use names as email addresses, on doors and desks, on name tags, and much more. Legally being allowed to change your name forces schools and workplaces to honor your chosen name. Additionally, it saves you a lot of stress and emotional trauma if you go to school or work at a company that is insensitive. Jace, who was a college student in Georgia, was in the process of changing his name legally when we spoke; however, he explained, "it's a little bit more of a process because my FAFSA [Free Application for Federal Student Aid], cause I'm a college student under my birth name, so, it's just been a very big process." Since Jace had completed his application for student aid under his prior name, if he legally changed his name it could cause major complications with his school records and financial aid. If schools would allow students to go by their chosen name, instead of their legal name, this wouldn't be as much of a problem, but many schools are behind the times and refuse to change emails, class rosters, and other systems that continue to use students' dead names and lead to a continuous attempt to get professors, staff, and other students to call them by their correct name.

This is why, despite the time, money, and effort needed to change your name, none of the respondents regretted their choice. In fact, many described the process as a lot easier than they had imagined it would be. Having legally changed my name (in the Midwest, not the South), I can say when it's over it definitely felt all worth it, but I do not want to paint a rosy picture of this process. Legally changing your name, especially in a conservative state, is a difficult and expensive process; consequently, it is also an exclusionary and class-based process that leaves trans people explaining their dead names, or having to go by them in certain places, like education and employment, even when they have chosen a name that fits them. Furthermore, changing your name is also a career, rather than a process, in the sense that it is never complete. Even though I legally changed my name in 2016, my dead name continues to haunt me to this day. My family and some of my friends from back home have still not gotten the hang of calling me Baker. Facebook, even with its endless list of gender identities, refuses to fix my name. I sent in my court order and my corrected driver's license, yet still Facebook shows my dead name in Messenger and when certain apps use my information. My college diplomas, hanging on my office wall still display my dead name because I'm too tired to go through the process of trying to get three Southern colleges and universities to change them. Maybe one day I will stop being dead named, but it hasn't happened yet, and I'm not holding my breath.

T & GENDER AFFIRMATION SURGERIES

Finally, physical transitioning, or what some refer to as biomedical intervention, was the third common experience for trans men in the South. For almost all of the respondents, physically transitioning their bodies to align more closely with their gender identities was an essential part of the process of becoming trans. In this section, I discuss the four most common biomedical interventions trans men undertook to better align their bodies with their identities: 1) hormone replacement therapy (HRT); 2) top surgeries; 3) bottom surgeries; and 4) hysterectomies.

Hormone Replacement Therapy

Almost all of the men were taking (43 of 51), or planned to take (7 of 51), testosterone to alter their bodies. Most respondents referred to it as "T" or as "HRT." Testosterone allows trans men to grow facial hair, reshape their bodies, and deepen their voices. Only one respondent, Max, an 18-year-old Hispanic pansexual male, said he was unsure if he would start HRT in the future, but he was waiting for now, because he would like to carry a child in the future.

Top Surgeries

Most of the respondents also had completed (19 of 51), or planned to complete (31 of 51), top surgeries. Top surgeries refer to a gender affirmation surgery to remove the breasts, and usually to restructure the chest to appear more masculine. Currently, there are two common top surgery procedures, the keyhole method and the double incision method. In general, the keyhole method is used for smaller breasts and removes the breast tissue through a "keyhole" incision at the bottom of the areola. The double incision method (or bilateral mastectomy) is a more invasive procedure that requires two larger incisions along the bottom of the breasts to remove the breast tissue, then the nipples are grafted back onto the chest in a way that gives a more masculine chest appearance. This procedure leaves larger scars, but the results today are better than ever before.

Many of the men felt that growing facial hair and having their breasts removed were the two most important physical components to being recognized as men. Levi, who had been dealing with insurance-related stalls with top surgery, said, "I have a lot of body image problems around my breasts, that's where my main dysphoria comes from. I want to be comfortable. I want to be able to feel the sun on my chest."

Again, only one of the 51 men I spoke with said they were not sure about whether they would have top surgery in the future. Dayton explained his conflict about whether or not to have top surgery:

> I'm not sure . . . it comes and goes . . . I mean there have definitely been times where, I'm like, yes, I definitely want top surgery, and sometimes I want both, bottom and top surgery . . . but then, you know, I also have the conflicting value of doing invasive things to my body . . . I feel like it's this internal conflict, I'm not really sure how to make sense of. . . . I'm like well would I want my body to change if others would love and accept me as I am? And . . . if it were legal for me to go shirtless and still be seen as a guy, or as not a girl . . . I probably wouldn't feel so strongly about. . . . On the other hand, I'm like . . . really wanting to fully experience, as much as technology allows, having a male body as much as I can. . . . Just because I feel like that's an experience that I . . . that feels like an expression of my inner truth, that doesn't get to be expressed.

Dayton was not the only person who struggled with this question of whether physical transition would be necessary, or at least necessary for so many trans people, if people would accept us for who we say we are. Having to choose between invasive surgeries and hormones for which the long-term effects are unknown, or having people recognize you as you recognize yourself is a double-edged sword. Neither option provides a good answer for many trans people. Yet, at least for the men I spoke with in the South, all but one were willing to risk the invasive surgery in order for the world to see them the way they saw themselves. This sentiment mirrors early work on trans men from Cromwell (1999, 106), who explicitly argues, "If breasts were defined as male, transmen and FTMs would not be dysphoric about them or have them removed. Because breasts are a sign of femininity, however, chest reconstructions are requested." I will return to this idea and explore it more fully in Chapter 3.

Bottom Surgeries

For trans men in this study, the next most common gender affirmation surgeries discussed were bottom surgeries—procedures to restructure the genitalia. Although this was the third most common procedure the men I spoke with sought, not a single respondent in this study had completed a bottom surgery. This was largely because the respondents felt the currently practiced procedures in the U.S. were too dangerous, too expensive, and often did not produce the results they desired. There are presently two common bottom surgery procedures for trans men: a phalloplasty (uses a skin graft from elsewhere on the body to construct a penis) or a metoidioplasty (releases existing tissue from the clitoris to construct a penis and sometimes involves rerouting the urethra to allow ease of urination while standing). In total, eleven of the 51 men I spoke with desired to have bottom surgery in the future and 18 were unsure if they would have the procedure (largely dependent on advances in technology and lower cost or insurance coverage). Six of the men said they would likely never have bottom surgery, and 16 said they did not plan to have bottom surgery.

Jamar did a lot of research on the various procedures and explained he wanted the least invasive surgeries possible in order to avoid losing sensation. Unfortunately, many of the men I spoke with felt the current surgeries available for trans men meant choosing between having a body that looked the way they wanted or losing sensation and sexual pleasure. For Jamar, maintaining his ability to feel pleasure was a top concern in choosing surgeries. When talking about bottom surgery, he explained:

> I want what I have naturally and I want to be able to feel it. If I sacrifice what feeling I have to make it look masculine, it's not worth it. It's just like when I get top surgery, I'm trying my best to get what they call key hole. . . . I won't lose sensitivity in my nipples, which is my biggest concern, cause with top surgery the biggest concern is if you lose your (A) sensitivity to the nipple, or (B) [the nipples] just fall off.

Given how advanced our medical technology is in the United States, it is indicative that these trans men in the South felt they were forced to choose between having their bodies look the way they wanted, and pleasure and safety. As one respondent explained, it is not an accident that the genital surgeries for trans women are able to safely and flawlessly create a vagina, yet trans men are still suffering and paying enormous amounts of money to have their breasts removed properly. Anytime a member of a subordinate group, in this case someone the world assumes is a woman, attempts to gain position in the dominant group, in this case a man, those with privilege attempt to ensure this does not happen.

This is why many of the men I talked to explained that bottom surgery was not currently up to their standards and they were hesitant to consider this option. Mason explained, "I don't foresee bottom surgery being what it needs to be in order, in my lifetime, for me to pursue that, but you know, other transmen certainly do. . . . For me the complications and the risks outweigh whatever personal gain I may have." Levi agreed:

> As far as bottom surgery, I doubt it. It's just not where it needs to be. I mean it's multiple surgeries and lots of down time for a non-functioning penis. Just to say, "I have a penis." For me, it's not worth it. Too much risk for not enough payoff. If I had it I would want a functioning penis, I can already pee standing up and there are devices for that without all those surgeries. I'll keep an eye on the process to see if it gets better, but for right now it's not in the cards for me. I don't need a penis to be a man.

Maddox, a 21-year-old white bisexual male who started testosterone the day of his interview, also said he was not planning to have bottom surgery "unless the technology, the surgery improves and is more effective." For Maddox, bottom surgery was "just kind of very expensive, you know, and you don't really get anything operable, you just have something for show." Colton agreed; he said that bottom surgery would cost too much and take him out of work for too long: "I don't know if it would be worth it. Especially for something that doesn't really work like a normal dude's would." Frank, a 41-year-old white straight male, put it this way: "What if it's aesthetically not what you are hoping for and you spend all this money and now you're bummed out because you know the whole you get what you pay for. So I just don't feel like I should butcher anything going on down there until you know . . . they come up with some standard outstanding surgery." Finally, Jeffrey, a 35-year-old white queer male, said the cost of bottom surgery is "exorbitant" and that he "couldn't justify taking that money away from my family."

Even for those respondents who wanted to have bottom surgery, it seemed like a distant and scary goal. Gordon, a 41-year-old white straight male, told me:

> Right now, it is my intent to do [bottom surgery] . . . I'm on the fence about it, but I want to have it, I'm just, you know, it's a scary process. . . . I want to have it, but it's not something I can do for several years, because of the cost. And I would have to travel out of state to get it done, which means, like a two- to three-week stay in another state.

Bruno said:

> As far as bottom surgery, I just have a lot of reservations for it. . . . With phalloplasty, they literally cut open the most sensitive part of your body. . . . I just don't want to pay for, you know, a penis that isn't gonna be aesthetically pleasing—not that any of them are—but that, you know, is weird looking, but you know I don't want mine to be extra weird looking. . . . It just doesn't seem like something that I would be satisfied with and, you know, there are prosthetics out there that I can pay a thousand dollars for and that are great and that you can't even tell are prosthetic. I don't have to go under a knife, and I don't have to have hair on my shaft.

Bruno expounded, because having a penis was not at the top of his priority list, "Why would I drop a thousand to have a wiener when I could drop a thousand dollars towards top surgery cause packing isn't very important to me." Derek also said he wasn't having bottom surgery right now because "I'm not at all satisfied with the current options. I guess I'm too picky. Being gay, or into guys, I know what a penis is supposed to look like and do and none of the options are even close."

It must be noted this is how the trans men in the South I spoke with felt about bottom surgeries; some of their opinions were based in fact—especially the high cost of the procedures; some of their opinions were based on anecdotal evidence—such as having friends or online acquittances who have had negative experiences with bottom surgeries; and some of their opinions were based on stereotypes about bottom surgeries and what a penis is supposed to look like and do. Many trans men in the U.S. do choose to have bottom surgeries, and those who do are generally happy with their decision (Cotten 2012). In addition, Cotten (2012) explains that trans men who choose bottom surgeries, despite the difficulties and complications that can arise, experience sexual pleasure, are pleased with the results, and are able to feel complete after the procedures.

Some respondents in this study were not interested in bottom surgery because they did not experience dysphoria around their genitals. For instance, Sage explained, "Bottom surgery does not really entice me whatsoever, uh, now that I've gotten the hang of it, I don't mind my bits so much. . . . There is something really nice about having a kind of, choose your own adventure every night." Donnie, a 28-year-old white pansexual trans male, said he just doesn't "feel enough dysphoria to warrant . . . a major surgery." Why this response is not more common among trans men in the South is likely due to notions of masculinity and cisnormative expectations of trans bodies in the region. Additionally, the trans men's reluctance to have bottom surgeries, when or if they are economically able to, was related to the construction of what a "good penis" looks like and does. Does a "good penis" need to look like a cis man's penis? For many of these respondents the answer was yes. Does a "good penis" have to perform and/or penetrate? Again, the construction of a penis for these men generally meant the answer to this question was yes. Therefore, trans men, and everyone, must continue to question the construction of a "good penis" and why anything less than this is a failure. This idea of a "good penis" harkens to constructions of intersexuality and the use of a phallometer to determine if a newborn meets the penile length threshold for maleness (see Davis [2015] for more on intersexuality).

Other Procedures for Gender Affirmation

Other men also mentioned additional procedures they had, or planned to have, for their transition. Following bottom surgery, a hysterectomy was the next most common procedure for the trans men in this study. In fact, seven of the trans men I talked with had already had the procedure completed. Additionally, ten planned to have a hysterectomy in the future, and three men said they would probably need the procedure due to the side effects of taking testosterone long-term. Theo wanted a hysterectomy because he said, "Eventually I'd wanna . . . get rid of all the extra parts I don't need. Like, hysterectomy and all that." Darius, a 23-year-old white asexual male, agreed; he would like to have a hysterectomy eventually, because "this uterus ain't doing nothing."

In addition to HRT, top and bottom surgeries, and hysterectomies, one respondent mentioned he would like to get liposuction on his hips, because even after being on testosterone and working to shape his body into a more masculine form, he still felt his hips were too wide and gave him a more feminine appearance. A few of the men discussed microblading, a semi-permanent tattoo procedure to fill out their eyebrows, or having thicker eyebrows tattooed on permanently in order to give their face a more masculine appearance. Lastly, one respondent said he was considering a vaginectomy (to remove the vagina), along with his metoidioplasty procedure.

CONCLUDING THOUGHTS

In this chapter, I examine three common experiences most of the men in this study dealt with in their process of becoming trans. Unmistakably, these processes varied greatly depending on the respondent's personality and intersecting characteristics; nonetheless, these common processes show some of the similarities in the experience of becoming trans men in the South. The three common experiences—1) coming out as trans to self; 2) choosing a name and legally changing your name; and 3) physically transitioning one's body to align with their gender identity—allow the reader to see many of the struggles trans people must deal with to be accepted as themselves. The goal of this chapter is not to satiate the reader's curiosity, or in any way be voyeuristic; rather, my intention is to allow the reader to gain empathy through education. By understanding the struggles of trans men in the South, and the lengths they must go to become themselves, I hope the reader feels the importance of understanding and making sure that all people have a choice to be themselves and the resources needed to accomplish that goal. Additionally, I hope this takes some of the pressure off of trans men to have to continue to explain their identities, names, and bodies to others, and puts some of the onus on others to take responsibility for educating themselves.

Chapter Two

Trans Manhood

Masculinities in the Southeast are highly intersectional and differ from masculinities in other regions of the country. Two factors that strongly influence the current versions of masculinities in the South are race and religion. As Friend (2009, xxiii) demonstrates, masculinity in the South is not merely the opposite of femininity, but "race, class, and sexuality are vital and equally influential factors as well, creating multiple masculinities." While these characteristics of masculinities vary and influence how masculinities are enacted, most scholars have ignored these and other important variables and continued to use a cisnormative lens. Studies of masculinities have largely focused on people who were assigned male at birth—based on the assumption that masculinities are a property of male bodies. In addition to using a cisnormative lens, geographic location is too often ignored in intersectional studies. These oversights lead researchers to paint uniform images of populations who vary greatly based on sex and geographic location. Regional constructions of masculinities in the South shape how trans men understand and do gender in the region. I demonstrate the importance of understanding the unique history of Southern masculinities and how this history influences trans men's understandings and enactments of gender. These findings are vital to a more comprehensive understanding of gender (specifically masculinities), the South, and how to address gender inequity in this region of the U.S.

MASCULINITIES AND MANHOOD ACTS IN THE SOUTH

Prior to the Civil War, white Southern men were defined by their honor and mastery over slaves and their families (Friend 2009). Following the Civil War, Southern men had to find new ways to define masculinity. One way they accomplished this was by setting themselves apart from "urban, indus-trial, liberal, corrupt, effeminate men of the North" (Friend 2009, x). This led to two dominant forms of manhood in the region—both of which continued to uphold "the old codes of honor and mastery" dominant during slavery: 1) the Christian gentleman—a man who was the "honorable, master of his household, humble, self-restrained, and above all, pious and faithful," and 2) the masculine martial ideal—a man who worshiped Confederate soldiers and modeled their masculinity after this "warrior-like and heroic manliness. . . . [in which] violence had to contain a broader and more ideological purpose, specifically to demonstrate honor in and protection of one's self, family, and region" (xi–xii). By World War I, a third form of manhood emerged in the South—"self-made manhood." This new form of masculinity "dissolved any possibility of 'race-neutral language' of masculinity and had elevated violence as the best means by which to preserve the racial status quo" (xvi).

In the early twentieth century, as the South became more and more evan-gelical, masculinity was again redefined to fit the changing conservative ide-als of the region. Honor was found in sports and hunting, but mastery "found a new home in religious visions of masculinity" (Friend 2009, xix). Evangeli-cals promoted an image of Jesus as muscular and hypermasculine and thought of religion as a holy crusade. This is also the period when homophobia was woven into the fabric of Southern masculinity. As Friend (xxi) puts it, "In the conservative South, homosexuality has always rubbed against the grain of masculinity. Viewing gay physicality as emasculating, white and black south-erners are very cautious about insinuations of homosocial activities taken too far." Overall, a Southern man is expected to be strong and aggressive, while simultaneously controlling himself and those under his protection, all while ensuring no one insinuates he is gay.

Examining how trans men in the South understand (trans)gender and "do gender" (West and Zimmerman 1987) allows for the exploration of masculin-ities and manhood acts that are not necessarily linked to male bodies. While masculinities are difficult to define (Pascoe and Bridges 2016; R. Connell 2005), most scholars agree masculinities are more than being male-bodied or some specific personality type. Masculinities are socially constructed and varied (Pascoe and Bridges 2016) and "inherently relational"—they exist in relation to femininities and other forms of masculinities (Friend 2009; R. Connell 2005, 68). Overall, masculinities are "collective forms of practice, belief, and interaction, which reproduce the subordination of women to men, and some men to others" (Sumerau 2012, 462). Through the subordination of women, all men gain "patriarchal dividends" (R. Connell 2005); enacting masculinities provides access to power and privilege in the current gender order. However, this power and privilege is not absolute. Often power and privilege are undermined or questioned due to marginalized (race, class, etc.) or subordinated (gay) identities (R. Connell 2005).

The difficulty in defining masculinities led Schrock and Schwalbe (2009) to propose the concept of manhood acts, which they argue more precisely defines the issues at the heart of masculinities research. Schrock and Schwalbe (2009, 280) suggest thinking of masculinities as plural can "make it hard to see what it is that masculinities have in common." Therefore, in order to understand masculinities, we must focus on how men "achieve dominance." According to Schrock and Schwalbe (2009, 281), "All manhood acts . . . are aimed at claiming privilege, eliciting deference, and resisting exploitation." Compensatory manhood acts are exaggerated performances of masculinity used to gain dominance by men who do not hold a hegemonic position in society (read white, able-bodied, cisgender, heterosexual, etc.). When people are unable to signify dominance because of marginalized characteristics, such as sexuality, race, ability, or immigration status, they engage in compensatory manhood acts to prove their masculinity (Ezzell 2012).

If the premise of manhood acts is accepted, then there is no healthy or inclusive version of manhood. To signify the possession of a masculine self (Schrock and Schwalbe 2009), trans men must participate in the dominance of men over women, and other men. As Ezzell (2016, 195) expounds, gender is inherently a category of inequality and doing manhood is always about being dominant; therefore, "you can't construct a masculinity or a definition of manhood that isn't predicated on inequality . . . although it is conceivable to construct and promote healthier masculinity for individual men, in the process we are still reinforcing larger structures of inequality by reinforcing the gender system." Thus, there is no way to overcome inequality within the current gender system (Ezzell 2016; Schrock and Schwalbe 2009). When trans men become men, they become part of the flawed system that expects and demands dominance of them.

In a few of the only studies to date that examine trans masculinities at the intersections of identity and geographic location, Abelson (2016a; 2019) finds that some trans men are able to gain acceptance as men through "claims of sameness." When trans men claim sameness with other men in terms of race (white), class (rural working-class), and sexuality (heterosexual), they can garner acceptance and gain access to the privileges of masculinity in the South and rural areas (Abelson 2016a). Place matters and is extremely important to understanding masculinities, especially regarding our "geographic imaginaries: the mental images we have of spaces and places that give them much of their meaning and that these places have produced in the popular imagination" (Abelson 2019, 28). Relatedly, trans men's feelings of safety and fear are vital to understanding how they practice masculinities (Abelson

2014). When trans men feel safer, they are more likely to practice transformative masculinities—meant to create gender equity—but when threatened, they practice defensive masculinities—more stereotypical displays of masculinity that uphold the domination of men (Abelson 2014).

Feelings of fear are magnified in the South, especially in rural areas (Abelson 2019; Rogers 2019a). The South in popular imagination is defined by a dichotomy between the Southern white man who is "bent on racial and patriarchal control, determined to protect white supremacy and white southern womanhood from any encroachment of blackness," and the "somewhat more benign good old boy" (Abelson 2019, 30). A specific type of good old boy that trans men associate with rural areas and the South is the redneck who "combines a rebelliousness and independence with a defense of traditional southern values. . . . [He] is a politically conservative, backward, and uneducated rural man wearing camo. . . . [He is] white, rural, heterosexual, and hypermasculine" (31–33). Both types of Southern masculinity can be dangerous for, or evoke fear in, trans men, especially trans men of color. Whether the respondents face any actual transphobic violence or not, "due to these fears . . . men were more likely to conform to local expectations of gender and sexuality and, for white trans men, to participate at least passively in systems of racial domination when interacting in rural settings" (Abelson 2019, 146). Conforming to local expectations and masculinities helps trans men avoid vulnerability and victimization, but simultaneously upholds the unequal gender system (Abelson 2016b). Consequently, examining trans masculinities in the South provides a view of the pressures of accountability trans men face in an oppressive, binary gender system, especially in the face of fear and violence.

FINDINGS: TRANS MANHOOD

Gender as Binary

Almost all of the men I spoke with provided a binary definition of gender. Most believed there are at least some essential differences between men and women. The idea that gender is socially constructed did not make sense to most of the men in this study, or they simply did not agree with this explanation. As Andre, a 33-year-old black straight trans male, put it, "I don't personally believe that gender is a social construct, because I personally believe in gender roles, not because they are forced, but when they are natural."

Many respondents focused on emotionality and sexuality as the main "natural" differences between men and women. Alec said there were differences between men and women, "especially mentally. . . . Women are naturally more emotional than men. . . . I think that's because they are made to mother children and birth children. Women are just built different than men; their brains work differently than men." A clear binary arose when the trans men in this region of the country spoke about differences between men and women. Liam believed "a patriarchal system is actually more stable and makes more sense." For these interviewees, gender differences were not bad or problematic, but were natural and helpful to the functioning of a society. Being placed into an incorrect gender identity at birth did not lead these men to believe gender was not natural, but instead showed that body parts are not the only determining factor of the essentialness of gender. Many respondents felt they needed to get their bodies, especially their hormones, in line with their own essential genders so that others could see on the outside what they felt on the inside.

The key to the binary distinctions between men and women for these re-spondents were hormones, specifically testosterone. Jayden, a 30-year-old white straight trans man, explained, "Obviously, testosterone and estrogen do completely two separate things in the makeup of the body." Before starting testosterone, Jayden said that the mention of "puppies or kitty cats or whatever and you get like excited and glee and yay and rainbows and butterflies. . . . I guess it's more of a controlled basis now, versus prior to hormones and so forth being a female." Likewise, Jamar believed testosterone led to more "dominant" traits in men; "like the rough and tumble, [men] like anything that can put out an aggressive outlet because of the way testosterone is," while "women tend to like more of an emotional connection." Whether sci-entifically testosterone and estrogen have these disparate effects is still up for debate, but the trans men in this study explained that there was a clear shift in their emotional life following testosterone. A lot of the respondents discussed not being able to cry anymore, along with more anger and aggression. At the same time, they also spoke of their emotions being more "controlled" now, which at least on the surface appears contradictory.

As for sexuality, respondents described a dramatic increase in sex drive after starting testosterone. Leo said his "sex drive is like that of a 14-year-old boy," and Derek concurred by saying "the volume on my sexuality is turned way up." Hayden, a 32-year-old multiracial pansexual male, explained that he started getting sexually aroused by "random objects" after starting testos-terone; he said this new sexual appetite "allowed me to understand a little bit more about where they used to say 'boys will be boys,' which is no excuse, but you know, I can look at a candle and get excited then there's no telling what else there is." Other respondents discussed that prior to testosterone they were mainly sexually attracted to one gender, but after testosterone they became more open to having sex with people of any gender, even if romanti-

cally their attraction did not change. Some of these changes resulted from
the respondents feeling more comfortable in their own bodies and identities;
however, some of this increased sex drive and attraction was chalked up to
the idea that men just want to have sex all the time, no matter who (or what)
it is with.

For respondents who viewed gender as a binary, the goal of transition was
to do gender "properly." Many explained that non-binary gender identities
did not make sense for them in their paradigm of gender. Being raised in the
South meant one was a man or a woman, and since they knew they were not
women, they must therefore be men. Jamar explained, "I think once you have
altered yourself some way, that you should be deemed the gender you are
trying to move to. I don't think you should have to go by trans anymore. . . .
I think the act of transitioning is the phase of going from one gender to the
other." Leo agreed: "I was brought up in a very conservative [environment]—
there's male and there's female, there's no trans this or that. So, in my head
there's still just male and female." Despite their experiences with gender,
they held firmly to the binary of male/man and female/woman. As Jamie, a
33-year-old white gay trans man, put it, "In the South, your gender role is one
of the most important things, like one of the biggest identifiers of your life. . . .
We all have grown up with that, there's very much a man's role and a woman's role in the home. It's hard to break free of that." With only two roles
available, the trans men I spoke with unquestionably chose man. As Jamie's
statement demonstrates, this choice was even more important in the South,
and in conservative areas of the country. Being trans did not necessarily make
it easier for many trans men to "break free" of certain aspects of gender socialization that had been ingrained in them since birth.

While most of the interviewees felt that gender was essential in at least
some ways, there were a few respondents who understood gender completely
as a social construct, without any basis in essential or biological differences.
For Mason, gender was based largely on stereotypes which "are institutions of
oppression . . . social constructs to keep one gender in power and one without.
As folks reclaim their power and their right to choose their own gender roles,
I think that will go away, but it's still socially what the norm is." Similarly,
Dayton felt that gender differences were "all societal norms. . . . I think that
every human has the capacity to a much wider range of ways of being in the
world than we ever thought possible, and I think that we're limited and a lot
of options are cut away in order to fit in the different boxes of social cultural
norms." Sage said, "Oh god, I fucking hate when people bring up spatial reasoning" as an essential difference. "[Society] encourages boys to play more
with blocks and run around and jump off shit, like no wonder they have better
spatial reasoning. I find it very frustrating. To me a lot of gender is so incred-

ibly socially constructed, and all the science is really fucking bad science." All of the respondents who explained gender fully as a social construct had learned about this in an academic setting and had worked in a helping profession with trans clients at some point. These views did not align with the other respondents in the South who had not worked with trans clients or who had not taken academic courses that explain gender as a social construct.

Defining Manhood

When it came to specifically defining manhood, many felt that manhood was whatever you wanted it to be, or an internal feeling that you are a man. They agreed with Alec: "Being a man is whatever definition you wanna give it. For me it's just being myself. I don't think that being a man necessarily has to have certain expectations or obligations." However, when it came to gender expressions and behaviors, most performed more stereotypical masculinities than their understandings of manhood might predict. Despite their initial responses of "just be yourself," many respondents clearly held specific ideas about how to do masculinity "properly."

Twenty of 51 trans men understood masculinity in a stereotypical and binary way. They defined masculinity in direct opposition to femininity, and discussed the importance of taking responsibility, protecting others, and lack of emotion to their versions of manhood. Jayden defined being a man as: "Being you and actually just taking ownership of what you do. . . . You need to be responsible for your actions. . . . In a man's position in society, it's always a place where people look up to you. . . . Being a man puts a lot of pressure or privilege [on you]." Along the same lines, Damien, a 38-year-old multiracial pansexual male, said being a man meant: "Being honest, and taking care of people, and owning up to mistakes, . . . and knowing when to step up and help protect somebody." Finally, Levi defined being a man this way: "It means to be privileged. It means to be taken more seriously. It means to be allowed to speak and be listened to. It means people turn to you for information and not to women." Clearly these respondents felt the privileges, and responsibilities, that came along with their versions of manhood; while they received the benefits of being listened to and taken more seriously, they must also take on the responsibility of protecting others and owning up to mistakes.

The other 31 trans men attempted to distance themselves from stereotypical and toxic versions of masculinity and manhood in some ways. These respondents provided more complicated definitions of manhood and appeared more self-reflective. For instance, Parker, a 23-year-old white trans masculine asexual person, explained that he wanted to identify as a man after transition, but through the transition process came to accept the trans part of his identity. At first, he believed, "Trans is just sort of the transportation from point A to point B and the end result will just be man. . . . As I've gone along the process of transitioning, I've gotten more comfortable with the idea of also being a man and being a trans person. . . . I feel better about embracing the trans part of it." Likewise, through his transition process, Samuel began to more fully understand the complexity of gender. He explained, "I've been medically transitioning for about five years now and my physical body isn't able to fit into either a male or female category and my identity, I feel, it isn't really ever going to fit into that. I don't have the kind of male socialization that makes me feel super comfortable around cis men." Finally, Billy, a 22-year-old white queer male, said, "I don't think I could ever identify just as male, because that isn't my experience. I identify as trans because I'm not ashamed of being trans. . . . I'm also like, I'm never going to look like a cis male." These respondents understood that their gender presentations would always fall short of the hegemonic understanding of masculinity, and therefore, they would be held accountable. Consequently, they decided rather than try to be recognized as cis men, they would take pride in their trans identity.

Doing Masculinities & Manhood Acts

Despite some flexible definitions of manhood, when it came to doing masculinities most trans men's gender expressions fit into stereotypical displays of Southern masculinity. Some of the respondents felt the need to engage in compensatory manhood acts, especially when their ability to "pass" as men was called into question or when they felt they were in vulnerable or dangerous positions—where being read as a woman or trans could lead to shaming or violence. In order to do masculinities, respondents stressed the importance of physical characteristics, such as having "a beard and lots of body hair" (Hugh, a 25-year-old white male) or "having more masculine qualities, like being kind of hairy and not having tits" (Liam), along with discussions about how to dress more masculine and lower their voices. Conversely, almost all the respondents were clear that being a man did not necessitate having a penis. As Hayden put it, being a man is "definitely not defined by the anatomy that you have and the little thing that's between your legs."

In terms of how a man acts, Mason said his version of manhood is "the guy who drinks whiskey and moonshine on the tailgate of his truck with his bird dog." Considering Abelson's findings about the importance of race to trans men's acceptance in the South, and rural areas particularly, it is worth noting that Mason was the only respondent who identified his race as Indigenous. It is possible that not being recognized as white meant that Mason had to engage in further acts of compensatory manhood in order to be accepted in the

South, especially in the rural area where he resided. This was also true of the other respondents in the study who identified as racial minorities. Not being able to claim sameness through race meant that other trans men who identified as black or Hispanic had to go above and beyond to have their manhood accepted, while simultaneously not appearing threatening.

Age also mattered when it came to doing masculinities. Jace, who was 18, adhered to a stereotypical definition of manhood and engaged in compensatory manhood acts, seemingly out of fear of not being recognized as a man. In his eyes, his age and having not completed his physical transition put him at a disadvantage in terms of being respected as a man. To Jace, being a man meant being physically strong, so he worked out and tried to shape his body to fit the stereotypes that aligned with his gender identity. Similarly, Rowen, a 22-year-old white straight male, said he "stands up taller; I try to make myself look a little bigger . . . so that I look a bit more masculine. I wear men's clothing, obviously. My hair is cut short . . . I'm getting facial hair . . . I pack [padding or a phallic object that gives the appearance of a penis or bulge] sometimes so that my body shape looks more masculine." Younger trans men worked hard to present a version of masculinity that was accepted and recognized as male through their physical appearance. These men often struggled to distance themselves fully from femininity until they began to be recognized as men more easily and felt more comfortable in their gender identity. Many trans men at the beginning of their transitions felt forced to "go all the way." However, once they felt more comfortable in their identities, some began to back off of the more stereotypical expressions of masculinities and to "just be themselves."

Another way respondents explained what it meant to be a man was through the stereotypical masculine roles they performed. For Nolan, "masculine characteristics involve outside work, making home repairs, all of that. . . . I have always modeled my own behavior, like most, based off of what I knew, and I grew up in a pretty rigid, you know, construct of male, stereotypical male and female social roles." Jeffrey also said his roles defined him: "Yes, I'm a guy, but I'm a father first and I'm a husband, and those things are much more important to me and how I see that a man should be." Along the same lines, Kevin, a 34-year-old multiracial pansexual male, defined being a man as being able to "do what you're supposed to do as a man for your wife." Interestingly, Kevin identified his sexuality as pansexual, but still saw being a man as taking care of a woman. Finally, Stuart, a 28-year-old white straight trans male, explained, "The man should be more the backbone and more the support and be the stronger half for the woman. . . . Where the woman should be taking care of the kids because they're gonna have more patience and more sympathy." These men cared deeply about the roles men were "supposed" to perform; men must be strong, mentally and physically, to take care of themselves, their families (usually described as women and children), and their communities.

Benevolent Sexism

When it came to doing masculinities and manhood acts, trans men often used benevolent sexism, rather than overt sexism, but the results were the same—domination of men over women. Benevolent sexism is defined as "the attribution of positive traits to women that, nonetheless, justify women's subordination to men" and frames women as "in need of assistance and protection from stronger, more physically powerful people (that is, men) . . . [and] by making women more dependent on men by virtue of positive characteristics attributed to femininity, ultimately positions women as inferior" (Wade and Ferree, 2019). This is an especially Southern manner of continuing gendered oppression through claims of chivalry and being a "Southern gentleman."

While the respondents tried to distance themselves from toxic masculinity, they fell into the trap of protection narratives. They did masculinities in a seemingly gentler manner—shaped by the norms of chivalry that are so heavily valued in the South—yet this continued to uphold a system of domination and oppression that privileged men over women. So, while trans men in the South largely continued to hold binary and essentialist understandings of gender, their region (and critical perspective on toxic cis masculinities) often led them to enact their masculinities in benevolent, rather than hostile ways.

For illustration, Liam said, "There's something that's more young about [women] because they are where youth comes from . . . something essentially like, you know, lively and youthful about [women] that men don't seem to have as much." While at first this may seem like a compliment, youth is often conflated with naivete and inexperience, and the assumption that women, who are youthful, need the assistance from men. In fact, Liam described being a man as, "I guess when someone's not being a man is when it mostly becomes apparent . . . if they're just like not being responsible or you know, acting childish," because being a man means "once he comes of age he starts acting responsibly." Therefore, the compliment of youthfulness Liam offered women was the very essence of unmanliness in his eyes.

Other respondents, especially those over 30, also demonstrated the importance of benevolent sexism to their understanding of doing masculinities. Frank, who was 41, discussed the importance of chivalry to his version of manhood; men "walk on . . . the street side of the sidewalk. I still hold doors open . . . I respect females as if they were my mother or sister." He continued, when a man is in public he must defend women "if someone would hit on them or do disrespect to them." Likewise, Ronald, who was 60, said he is "an Alpha-male, a leader. . . . I'm not a misogynist or sexist or anything like that. I treat women like queens. I'm a heterosexual male. I love women. . . . I've always been a provider, even when I was a woman, but now I feel like I can do that better." These quotes demonstrate the importance of benevolent sexism to upholding men's privileged positions. While masculinity was a difficult concept to explain for many respondents, several jumped immediately to superiority over women as the best explanation of what it meant to be a man. For these men, compensatory manhood acts of chivalry and taking care of women were necessary components of validating their claims of manhood and masculinity in the South.

Some of the men tried to figure out how to be accepted and recognized as men, while at the same time not bringing all of the problematic and oppressive elements of manhood with them. For instance, Gordon said manhood meant: "Taking care of your family, but still being kind and gentle. . . . You don't have to be so masculine that you're an ass." However, he explained, "some sides of myself I'm not comfortable leaving exposed, like my emotions. . . . I just feel like I have to be a hard ass at times. And because I've created that image I can't really show anything other than that." The balance between being recognized as a man in the South, while not being toxic turns out to be extremely difficult, especially when manhood is fundamentally defined as having control and power over others. Some respondents continued to grapple with the question of whether there can be a healthier and gentler masculinity, or if they will have to give up being recognized as men in order to escape the toxicity of masculinity.

CONCLUDING THOUGHTS

Overall, the expectations of being a man for trans men in the Southeastern U.S. are not that different from those placed on cis men in the region. Over time, many trans men in the South came to embrace these expectations and engaged in stereotypical performances of masculinities. They felt presenting stereotypical masculinities was desirable, or at least required in some situations, for living as a trans man in the South. Despite prior experiences being recognized as girls/women, following transition many respondents felt that being a man meant taking care of women. Making sense of a system that justifies subordination of women was difficult for some respondents, but many fell into their new position as members of the dominant group seemingly without discordance. Of course, none of the men wanted to be viewed as sexist, and thus treaded lightly on the subject of men's superiority over women. Nevertheless, their benevolent sexism is just as damaging as overt and hostile sexism; assuming women need men's assistance—because women are weaker and more emotional—continues to give men power over women. In the South's culture of politeness and chivalry, when women object to benevolent sexism they are told to smile and take the help or the compliment.

These findings support the notion that manhood equals dominance. Trans men have been socialized in a culture where masculinities are defined as dominance, and they have been unable to find another way to do manhood that does not continue to oppress women and is not predicated on inequality. Based on this evidence, Ezzell (2016) is correct that masculinities by definition cannot be healthy or inclusive. Like cis men, trans men in the South have been unable to find a way to enact masculinities that are not based on inequality. While benevolent sexism, and some more open ideas about gender, may make trans men's masculinities gentler, as Ezzell (2016) states, "a kinder, gentler patriarchy is *still* patriarchy."

Trans men's enactments of masculinities are part of a flawed gender system—patriarchy—not individual flaws of trans men (Pfeffer 2017). While a higher moral responsibility for challenging toxic masculinities cannot be placed on trans men, masculinities and manhood acts must be critiqued in all forms in order to overcome inequality. Moving forward, scholars and activists must find a way to critique trans men's masculinities, without critiquing trans men themselves for trying to fit into an oppressive system. Simultaneously, the dangers of living as a trans person in the South must be kept at the forefront of conversations. Trans men cannot be expected to avoid all of the negative implications of masculinities and inequalities in the South; however, they also cannot be valorized as a group of men who are somehow better for equality than cis men. Just like all masculinities, trans masculinities can be toxic and can harm women and other men.

Chapter Three

Born in the Wrong Body

As discussed in Chapter 1, medical intervention is an important part of transition for some trans people, but "the privileging of this model over others creates a marginalizing effect for gender-non-conforming people who cannot or do not wish to medically transition" (Johnson 2016, 466). Transnormativity, according to Johnson (2016, 466),

> is a hegemonic ideology that structures transgender experience, identification, and narratives into a hierarchy of legitimacy that is dependent upon a binary medical model and its accompanying standards, regardless of individual transgender people's interest in or intention to undertake medical pathways to transition.

Additionally, medicalization— "the process by which human problems come under control of medical authority and become classified as something to be diagnosed, treated and potentially cured"—allows medical authorities social control over identities and behaviors viewed as deviant in our society (Johnson 2019, 518).

Through an analysis of narratives of trans men in documentary films, Johnson (2016, 468) argues that trans people are held accountable to transnormative standards which are "reliant on . . . adherence to a medical model of transition that emphasizes a *born in the wrong body* discourse and a *discovery narrative* of trans identity." Relying on a medical model of trans identity and experience means that trans people must have been "born this way" to be authentic, to really be trans. If a person is "born in the wrong body," what follows must be a narrative of "discovery"—a story of realizing one's transness and that this is the way you've always been.

Catalano (2015) also examines these transnormative expectations in their article "Trans Enough?" Catalano argues, along with Cromwell (1999, 413), that the born in the wrong body narrative "is a superficial description for the misalignment between body and cultural meanings of gender ascribed to specific parts of the body." That is, if we did not assume that certain body parts only belonged to certain types of bodies, this idea of born in the wrong body would not make sense; this description of trans identities is completely grounded in a binary sex and gender system.

In a subsequent ethnographic study of mostly younger (under the age of 34) trans people, Johnson (2019) reveal that many trans people are beginning to move away from the medicalized narrative of transnormativity in their understanding of what it means to be trans. In his ethnographic work at an annual summer camp for young trans people, Johnson (2019, 522) finds that most of the "members of the group largely dismissed the classification of gender dysphoria as a medical condition, specifically a psychological disorder." Despite moving away from a medicalized model of trans identity, the participants in Johnson's study continued to stress "the importance of access to medical intervention for those who want it" (2019, 524). Overall, the medicalization of trans identities is a complex issue. On the one hand, trans people do not want to be viewed as having a disorder and the stigma that comes along with a mental health diagnosis in the United States. However, in order to access medical interventions, such as hormone therapy and gender affirmation surgeries, a diagnosis is required. Johnson (2016, 487) suggests that "future research should continue to explore this phenomenon [of transnormativity] in the everyday lived experiences of transgender people."

By exploring how Southern trans men uphold or reject transnormative ideology and medicalization in their lives, I expand on the concept of transnormativity. I explore whether these men hold a queerer understanding of what it means to be trans than transnormative narratives allow. By a queerer understanding, I mean discussing and thinking about gender outside of the binaries of female/male, masculine/feminine, woman/man, and outside of the medical model. Or, do trans men in the South reinforce a transnormative narrative by adhering to "medicalized regulatory standards placed on their identities" (Johnson 2016, 466)?

West and Zimmerman (1987) show that everyone is held accountable to doing gender according to hegemonic standards of what it means to be a man and a woman. As Johnson (2019, 525) argues:

> Gender affirming medical interventions do more than validate trans people's identities, they ease the social interactions wherein trans people are expected to *do gender* by adhering to preconceived notions of what men and women look and sound like. . . . The risks of violence, aggression, harassment and discrimination are more prevalent for trans people who are recognized as trans or

gender diverse. Medical intervention is thus necessary for many trans people's quality of life.

Medicalization and narratives of born in the wrong body and discovery are vital to many Southern trans men's everyday lived experiences. Medical intervention allows some trans men to "fit" into the gender binary and live more comfortably and safely in the South. Consequently, I examine how strictly trans men in the South adhere to these narratives, and if they use transnormative standards to hold other trans people accountable to what it means to be trans. Do trans men in the South see medical transition as superior to other forms of transition? Or do they employ the medical model only as "a specific frame to translate personal experience to others in language they can understand," or because "society at large respects medical authority over personal experience" (526)?

Another important aspect of transnormativity and the medicalization of becoming trans is that this gatekeeping leads to extreme inequality, especially in terms of socioeconomic status. In order to fit into the transnormative narrative, trans people must have the material resources, ability, and understanding of the narrative to engage in medical intervention. Additionally, as Johnson (2019, 528) explains,

> Strategic engagement with medical authority may not be equally available to all trans people in all contexts. The power of trans people to lean on the diagnostic category as a strategic tool requires an understanding of the expected narratives, an audience that respects medical authority, and the credibility to be positioned as an authority of one's own experiences within medicalized contexts.

These tools and credibility rely on multiple intersecting characteristics, including, but not limited to, class, race, ethnicity, ability, and education. Research has already begun to show that "nonbinary trans people and trans people of color may not be positioned to benefit from strategic engagement with medical authority as much or in the same ways as white trans people who identify within the gender binary" (529). Does this mean that trans men of color, poor trans men, and others marginalized by intersecting characteristics in the trans community are more likely to reject the medical model?

These discovery narratives in childhood and adolescence are especially important when considering that psychiatrists and medical doctors continue to act as gatekeepers for a diagnosis of gender dysphoria (Johnson 2015), which is necessary in order to receive medical intervention and for insurance coverage of hormones and surgeries (which most insurance still does not cover). This is why "trans people have employed various tactics and strategies to become recognizable to medical gatekeepers, such as constructing narratives to meet requirements that do not fully reflect their lived experiences" (Catalano 2015, 414; Rubin 2003).

According to the Diagnostic and Statistical Manual (DSM-5) of Mental Disorders (2013), to be diagnosed with gender dysphoria, children must demonstrate "a marked incongruence between one's experienced/expressed gender and assigned gender." To meet this criterion, the DSM-5 states that a child must meet six of eight criteria for a period of at least six months. The eight criteria are (DSM-5 2013):

1. A strong desire to be the other gender or an insistence that one is the other gender (or some alternative gender different from one's assigned gender).
2. In boys (assigned gender), a strong preference for cross-dressing or simulating female attire; on in girls (assigned gender), a strong preference for wearing only typical masculine clothing and a strong resistance to wearing of typical feminine clothing.
3. A strong preference for cross-gender roles in make-believe play or fantasy play.
4. A strong preference for toys, games, or activities stereotypically used or engaged in by the other gender.
5. A strong preference for playmates of the other gender.
6. In boys (assigned gender), a strong rejection of typically masculine toys, games, and activities and a strong avoidance of rough-and-tumble play; or in girls (assigned gender), a strong rejection of typically feminine toys, games, or activities.
7. A strong dislike of one's sexual anatomy.
8. A strong desire for the primary and/or secondary sex characteristics that match one's experienced gender.

To be diagnosed with gender dysphoria, children must also demonstrate that these "symptoms" are "associated with clinically significant distress or impairment in social, school, or other important areas of functioning" (DSM-5 2013). Therefore, in order to have a "valid" discovery narrative, many trans men use these criteria as signs that they have always been trans. This is not to imply that trans people are lying about their experiences; rather, it shows the importance of medicalization and gatekeeping for trans identities. Why should it be necessary to reject all things feminine or prefer playing with the boys (who get to play more fun games anyways) to have your identity validated? Why must you be an *extreme* tomboy or worried about your genitalia at such an early age to *prove* you are trans? These diagnostic criterion show the absurdity of having to prove your identity to someone else. They display the absurdity of having to prove a "gender troubled childhood" in order to access medical interventions (Spade 2003, 23). They demonstrate that being trans is not a medical condition, but rather a social identity.

Nevertheless, medicalization is powerful, and trans people know that in order to receive medical intervention, if that is what they desire, they have to fit into the medical box that gender dysphoria has created for them. As many trans people move away from the medical model of trans identities (Johnson 2019), they continue to understand the importance of this model for receiving care and for explaining their identities to others who choose not to believe them without *proof* that it is "natural" or "essential." As Samuel put it, "I think they take me more seriously about trans stuff now than they did before I passed, because . . . they see me more as like, oh, he's an expert now, he's done it, he's already gone through it . . . because to them, all trans people want to medically transition and stuff." If people are ignorant of the diversity of trans people and their desire, or lack thereof, to have medical intervention, then it becomes easier in some ways for trans men to pass as cis and shape their narratives in ways that medical providers may understand.

The problem is that these narratives leave "very little room for trans people's faculty or power to use their own agency in making decisions about their identification with and actualization of their individual gender identities" (Johnson 2016, 469). At the same time, these narratives allow many trans people, especially in areas or groups where being trans is not understood, to be accepted because they've "always been that way." "Born this way" narratives are particularly important in regard to conservative religions—if God made you the way you are, then it must be right. Previous research demonstrates that Christians' perceptions of the origins of an identity or behavior are strong predictors of beliefs and attitudes toward individuals who they view as being outside of the norm. That is, if Christians, especially mainline Protestants and liberal Catholics, believe an identity, such as gay, lesbian, or trans, can be controlled or changed by the individual, they are more likely to hold negative attitudes about that identity and the individual who continues to identify in ways they do not agree with or engage in behavior that they view as deviant (Baker and Brauner-Otto 2015; Whitley Jr. 2009).

Critiquing the coexisting narratives of "born in the wrong body" and "discovery" is not a critique of trans people who feel they were born in the wrong body, or realized they had always been trans. Rather, critiquing these narratives allows us to break down transnormative assumptions that to "really" be trans you must have been born that way and discover that you always felt like you were in the wrong body. This is a critique of a normative system, which establishes a hierarchy of what is more valid and real, and not of any individual's narrative or understanding of their own experiences. Also, questioning the ubiquitousness of these narratives for trans people can empower those who do not identify with these narratives (such as non-binary people or trans people who do not wish to transition physically) and can reduce therapists' and medical providers' gatekeeping abilities if there is more than one valid way to be trans.

FINDINGS: "BORN IN THE WRONG BODY" & THE "DISCOVERY" NARRATIVE

The vast majority of respondents continued to use the "born in the wrong body" (20 of 51) and "discovery" (50 of 51) narratives to describe their experience of being trans. As Jace described, "We're *trapped in female bodies* for the time being, but we are men. . . . It's just something that we are, like, mentally, *we've always been*, but we've just never been able to categorize it and figure out what it was" (emphasis mine). Comparably, Theo simply said, "I was born female and I thought that was my identity and then *discovered* later that wasn't correct" (emphasis mine). While most respondents felt that being "born in the wrong body" was just a mistake, Andre believed there was a purpose for trans people being born in the wrong body; he believed that being trans allowed people to have empathy in a way that cis people were unable to. Andre explained, "I was born in a woman's body in order to learn a specific experience . . . I was always *born a male in a woman's body* and socialized as a woman. You know, just to learn how to be balanced as a human being. I learned to have compassion for both males and females" (emphasis mine).

On the contrary, Zac, a 20-year-old white bisexual FTM person, said, "I don't like saying that I'm in the wrong body. This is just the body that I have and this is the body that I'm working with." He described being trans as "a really big internal struggle with your gender wondering whether or not you've been assigned the right one and just kind of feeling like everything's all wrong, like your body and your mind don't really line up." While Zac understood some of the problems with the "born in the wrong" body narrative, he still felt that there was somehow an essential mix-up between his mind and body. While his body may not be wrong per se, someone messed up when they classified it as female.

Most respondents said they always knew they were trans, but it took time to put the pieces together. Alec explained, "I think for me it might've been something that I always knew. . . . I think it was always there in the back of my head. I started looking back at my childhood and the things that I went through and the different feelings that I could remember having as a kid, and it just kinda fit." Gordon always knew he was different also; he explained he "didn't really fall into any quote-unquote normal category." Gordon described it this way:

Growing up, I was a huge tomboy. Like the biggest tomboy you would've ever seen. And when I was younger I would do a lot of things that some people would consider typical for a trans man, in that, I would take a rolled up pair of socks and put it in my underwear, or I always wanted to play the boy parts when I was playing with friends, and I always wanted the boy toys, I didn't like baby dolls or Barbie or any of that stuff. . . . I've always wanted to know what it was like to have a penis; since I was little. And I just didn't like girl stuff, I never liked girl stuff.

Many of the men described themselves as being beyond "just a tomboy." Garrett, a 22-year-old white pansexual trans guy, said, "Through childhood . . . all I wanted to do was wear boy shorts and go out there without a shirt while I'm swimming. . . . I just thought that was just like a normal tomboy thing, but I'm like, 'Oh, wait. That's not it.'" These respondents used their extreme dislike for "girl stuff" as evidence they were never meant to be a woman. Damien said, "I mean I just always played with cars and trucks and I would dress up as Rambo when I was a kid, and it just felt right." Likewise, Samuel told me about playing boy characters while growing up:

My favorite thing to do when I was growing up was I would role-play on the Neopets [a virtual pet community] where you would like make up a character and you would write stories of people where you would like play . . . a character or a couple of characters and you would just have them interact with each other and I always played a boy and I hated playing a girl. . . . I very quickly gravitated to playing a boy and wouldn't do anything else, but that wasn't even enough for me where I wanted not only for my characters to be boys, but I wanted the people I was playing, role-playing with to see me as a boy, and so I would also like be playing these boy characters and also telling them I was a boy and my name was like Mike or all these other names.

Role-playing as a boy and pretending to be a boy in online communities came up often in the interviews. Jamie said he always wanted to be male characters when he would "play make-believe" or video games; he explained, "I never really identified with the female characters."

Like other trans men in this study, Jamie was able to discover and explore his trans identity through drag, which could be viewed as a type of role-playing as well. As I've demonstrated in other work (Baker and Kelly 2016; Rogers 2018a), drag kinging is a common way for trans men to learn about their identity and how to be a man in the South. Jamie explained, "I started doing drag and being this male character, and really felt like a lot of things that I had struggled with as far as my confidence, or my ability to be outgoing, or even just like my ability to like myself, sort of started to fade away any time that I was in that character." Drag kinging allows many trans men to play with gender in a safe environment while they figure out what type of gender expression and identities fit them best. This supports my previous findings of the importance of drag kinging as a resource for trans and non-binary people in the Southeast, where other resources are often limited, and in small cities and rural areas sometimes wholly absent.

While for some trans men discovery was a process that took place over an extended period of time, other respondents pinpointed a specific time or incident that led to their discovery of their trans identity. For instance, Maddox explained his discovery as a process over time. He said he was 17 when he learned what it meant to be trans and that trans described how he felt. Friends and families also took part in helping trans people to construct these narratives of "born in the wrong body" and "discovery." Maddox said his childhood memories were "pretty fuzzy," due to having a tumor removed from his head at the age of 16, but said that his mom told him stories that prove he was always trans: "My mom told me that from like a little kid, like, could talk age, I would insist that I was a boy, and of course, you know, they always shot it down."

Generally, the stories the men shared with me occurred in two distinct time periods: 1) around the age of two or three, and 2) around the age of seven or eight. According to Travers (2018, 16), "Research and anecdotal evidence indicates that children have a strong sense of their own gender identity by the age of three or four and some earlier than that." Travers explains that "[c]hildren are not blank slates, as early approaches to child development and education insisted, but rather are fundamentally social beings who strive for the agency to construct themselves as much as they are constructed by inter-actions with people and institutions around them" (17). In Meadow's (2018) study of trans kids, parents began to suspect that their female assigned child was trans masculine, or to see the child's masculine behaviors as problematic around age ten. The two time periods during which the men in this study began to understand their own identities aligns with previous research. Around the age of two or three, the men began to understand their own identity, but usu-ally concealed it due to lack of support. Then again, around the age of seven or eight, the differences between themselves and other girls began to become more evident. Hence, parents may start to catch on around age ten for trans boys because "the disproportionate value placed on normative masculinity al-lowed boyish girls far more latitude to display gender nonnormativity than it did for boys who display devalued feminine traits" (Meadow 2018, 46). This is why parents "seldom sought support for masculine behavior in girls absent an extreme degree of emotional distress or a persistent male identity" (47).

Nolan discussed his earliest memory of being trans. He told me about a memory he had of knowing he was born in the wrong body:

> I have never really fluctuated in my gender identity. I've known, I mean, I've got memories of being in diapers and knowing something wasn't right. But there was never a fluctuation, I've adamantly always been male identified. . . . I was probably two years old or something and I was having my diaper changed in front of female friends of my mom's and I just remember feeling ashamed. I didn't really understand why, but I remember hating to have my diaper changed in front of people 'cause something just didn't feel right. It's a little weird 'cause I can even tell you the color of the washcloth, it's so funny, I remember vivid details.

While Nolan's memory may not have literally happened when he was two, "[e]arliest memories also are an important source of 'evidence' for a temporally continuous sense of self (Bauer, Tasdemir-Ozdes, and Larkina 2014, 83). That is, we recognize ourselves as the same person over time because we remember events from our past." This may account for why these memories at such a young age stand out for trans men; these memories help them to tell their story of discovery and draw a path from their young self to their self today.

Andre also said he was two or three when he realized he was trans. When his mom's friends referred to him as her son, she would correct them and tell them that he was her daughter, but he knew at this early age that didn't feel right. At the age of three, Walker remembered saying he was a boy. He said, after that "they had to convince me otherwise," which they tried to do through therapy, "but at age three, I already knew that I was male or identified as male." Jorge said that when he was three, "I told everybody that I was male and they had to call me Jackson and I would not answer to anything else." Dakota's discovery began around age three and was crystalized later around age eight:

> Honestly, like as far as when I first started to mention [I was meant to be a boy] . . . I was three. My mom just said that every time they would put me in like a little dress or whatever I would freak out. . . . I would always yell at them and say, "No, I'm a boy. Why are you putting me in a dress?" And I would cry and scream until they changed me.

Especially at such a young age, most parents did not believe or support their children's claims that they were not the gender that aligned with the sex they were assigned at birth. Travers (2018, 17) explains that even today the "prevailing attitudes about children and teenagers allow adults to dismiss statements that young people make about themselves and the world around them." Additionally, because all of the respondents identified as masculine, their parents likely were not that concerned: "Transboys . . . have much greater latitude to exhibit their masculinity without adults considering it a problem warranting attention or outside support" (Meadow 2018, 50).

While most of the earlier memories took place in relation to family, the memories from age seven or eight often occurred in interaction with peers and friends. Gabriel was eight when he realized he was trans: "The earliest time I can pinpoint feeling that way was in like third grade, so like 8 years old, and I was running around with a friend of mine and she kinda made some comment about me being a tomboy, and I was like, 'Well, I am a boy.'" Bruno also had a specific moment when he realized he was trans: "I've always realized, like, that I didn't feel right. . . . There was obviously that little bit of *discovery* process for me" (emphasis mine). He described the moment when it all came together for him at the age of eight, when he realized "something was like woah, what's going on?":

> When you first start to grow breasts, your nipple areola complex like comes, like, it hardens and so like you'll still be flat chested, but you'll get like really sensitive, and I was skateboarding and I fell, and I just fell like chest first going down this hill and it hurt and I was like, "Oh, no!" those are gonna be breasts and I just started crying. And I didn't know why I was so upset about it, but that was like the first time that I was like, how's my body gonna look?

Bruno explained that at the age of eight he didn't know "trans people existed," but the day he found out he came out as trans. Similarly, Donnie remembered when he was "very young . . . like as soon as I was aware of . . . the differences between boys and girls, basically, I just remember that I really wanted a penis." He wasn't "super unhappy as a girl," but the more he performed masculinity, the more comfortable he felt and eventually he no longer felt comfortable as a woman. While Dakota started mentioning he was a boy at three, he continued his discovery narrative with a story from when he was around seven:

> Then, as I got older . . . my first best friend, I was seven years old and I actually met him, because he moved in next door and I was on the front porch, sweeping the front porch, because my mom told me to. And I was wearing jean shorts and no shirt. But at seven years old like, you know, like I looked like a little boy out there, you know, a biological boy out there sweeping the porch and my mom said she looked out the big bay window and I was standing there talking to him. And she yelled at me to come put a shirt on . . . whenever I came in, she said that we had this big blowup fight, because she kept telling me, "No, little girls have to wear shirts. You can't go out outside without a shirt on." And she said I just kept yelling at her, "But I'm not a girl. I'm not a girl. What are you talking about?" . . . That's just my earliest memory is seven years old, being on the front porch like, "Oh, I'm sweeping the porch. I'm doing fine without a shirt on," and her yelling at me and me not understanding why.

Many of the men were sure they were boys by the age of seven or eight, but their parents were often not ready to deal with this issue. Therefore, most of the men were dismissed and forced to hide their identities until they were older and could figure out what was going on for themselves.

Even those who did not feel like their stories lined up with the "born in the wrong body" and "discovery" narratives understood the importance of these narratives. Derek explained that he didn't realize he was a man until his mid-teens: "I didn't know when I was a kid like a lot of people, but once I was in high school, I started to feel different." For Derek, being trans meant, "someone who is assigned a gender at birth, but at some point identifies with a gender other than the gender they were assigned. . . . For me, I describe being trans 'strictly as an annoying medical condition.'" Although he did not feel he was born in the wrong body or discovered his trans identity, he felt the medical model was the best explanation for his trans identity, and that this medical condition, like any other, could be onset at any point in your life.

Intersecting Identities and Discoveries

Each discovery narrative took place in a specific geographical location, time, and at the intersections of a variety of other identities. Some of the trans men explicitly pointed out these intersections, and how discovering and coming to terms with their trans identities was complicated by other systems of oppression. For instance, Jayden's discovery narrative revealed how his sexuality and gender identity were intertwined. Growing up he would always look at men and think, "Wow, you know, he has really nice form . . . really nice structure." He wasn't attracted to men in the same way he was attracted to women; rather, he said, as "I understood myself more and the reasons why I was never really attracted to men . . . I really came to find out it was because I feel like I always wanted to be that man, or to be something like those men . . . I would have, not an attraction, but an expression to them." When Jayden first came out, he came out as a lesbian:

> I think the main reason I was living a life that way was because I didn't know of transgender. I did not come to my transitional point until I met a trans man . . . from that point, it kinda just connected all the dots and put together the pieces that were never there before, so I did live the life of a lesbian, happy, proud, gay, um, still happy, proud, gay, just not living life as a lesbian [now].

Being 30 years old, Jayden did not have the type of media influence and role models that trans kids today can often see on TV. He did not know what transgender was when he started to realize something didn't feel right about his identity. This took place well before we reached the "transgender tipping point" (Steinmetz 2014), when "images of adults who elect to change their social gender categories [became] a mainstay of media discourse" (Meadow 2018, 3).

As Jayden connected his gender identity to his sexuality and attraction, Jamar linked his to his biological sex. Jamar believed he was born intersex, but his mom would not confirm this. Jamar told me, "There is a probability that I may have actually been intersex, when I was born, because I have two unexplainable scars that, the only time those scars are done like that is when the testicles are removed. . . . So, there's a high speculation that I was, and I remember seeing a picture when I was real little of a baby boy, and it had my name on the back." When he found the picture, his mom grabbed it from him and threw it in a fire. He said, "I think she made a decision and that's the decision she wanted it to be, and she was ashamed about her decision, cause I think me wanting to be a boy, I think it ate at her." Even if his mom would not confirm that he was born intersex, Jamar said, "I feel like I am a boy. I was born a boy, even though I was born in a female body."

For Leo, a straight black male, his race was a key component of his discovery narrative. In a joking manner, Leo told me he always thought he was "really weird" because "I always thought I was gonna grow up and I can change. . . . I was gonna be a white boy that became a country singer. Like, that's my dream as a child. It didn't happen; I was really disappointed about that." Leo held such a specific version of the type of masculinity he wanted to embody that he believed not only did he need to transition to be a man, but also to be white. He did not see other black country music singers at the time, so to fit the mold of masculinity he felt was most true to himself, he had to become white, and a country music singer. The importance of role models came up again and again. As Leo explained, he thought he would need to change his gender and race to be the type of country music singer he aspired to be. Similarly, most trans men had a hard time imagining themselves as men at first because they had no trans role models to show them the way. This is why some respondents specifically identified as trans and sought to be role models for younger trans people; they wanted younger trans men to be able to see what was possible and have someone who could help them along the way.

Another factor that had a major influence on trans men's discovery narratives was age. Most interviewees always felt they were trans but did not have the language to describe it when they first discovered something was different about them. Now that the language of trans identities is much more widely known, trans people can be seen in the media, and the internet offers endless information about being trans, discovery of one's trans identity is often a much faster process than it was for the older men in this study. Not knowing there is a term for your identity makes it almost impossible to explain to others. Without an identity label, many people are led to believe that no one else feels the way they do. Having a concept for who you are can make people feel like they are part of a group, or at least that there are other people who feel similar to them, which can be comforting.

At 41 years old, Frank recalled his discovery process taking a long time, because he didn't know what trans was until he saw Chaz Bono on TV. Frank was not the only man I spoke with who mentioned that they did not know it was possible to be a trans man until seeing the coverage of Chaz's transition (recall Ronald's coming out story from Chapter 1). Since Frank was young, people always called him a tomboy, but something didn't feel right about that label. Frank described how the uniform at his Catholic school led him to believe that something else might be going on:

> I went to private school, a Catholic school, so females are required to wear, sort of, jumpers or whatever, like a little skirt, a little plaid skirt. . . . So, I always would wear like running shorts or basketball shorts underneath it because it felt comfortable. And I had an older sister and . . . because people . . . I had a shorter haircut growing up, they're like, "Oh, there's your little brother," and I would not take offense and I'd actually be proud that somebody, you know, misgendered me and then, "Oh no, this is . . . my little sister." And then I'd get kind of grumpy that, you know, they corrected them. So, I think I knew somewhat . . . I wasn't quite a tomboy, but I didn't know that there's anything in order to identify that.

After that, Frank assumed he was a lesbian, because he liked women, until he realized that trans was an identity. Frank's discovery was related to both age and sexuality.

While almost all of the men I spoke with gave a discovery narrative of some sort, and most felt they were born in the wrong body, one respondent explicitly rejected these narratives. Sage, a full-time student and a graduate assistant in an LGBTQ student center, said:

> I identified very strongly as a woman, I wanna say like . . . middle of middle school going backwards. . . . Like I have very strong memories of like, "No, I'm a girl and I'm gonna make it." So, I don't really kind of ascribe to the born this way, like, I was always a man. I don't want to degender my past self and those feelings I had, but I would consider myself identifying much more neutrally or in a state of confusion during like the last half of high school.

Sage's thoughts here are likely related to his education and work in an LGTBQ student center. In his privileged position as a white trans man working on a master's degree, Sage did not have to claim the "born in the wrong body" and "discovery" narratives to be taken seriously.

HIERARCHY OF TRANSNESS

Although most respondents adhered to transnormative narratives, and some had personally felt the effects of transnormativity on their lives, the majority did not seem to hold transnormative beliefs about a right, or correct, way to be trans. Just because their trans identity fit the accepted narratives didn't mean that everyone else's did, or needed to. Almost all of the respondents felt that access to medical interventions for trans people was an important resource if desired; however, they were clear to say that choosing to medically transition did not make someone more or less trans. Most felt that medically transitioning was an individual and personal decision that each person must make based on their own desires and resources.

As Theo said, "I think it's everyone's own decision. I don't feel like they have to have [surgery] to prove anything. . . . If they don't wanna do it for whatever reason, whether that be cost or just not a part of their transition . . . I don't look at them differently." Mason felt similar to Theo, but thought that physical transition should be an option for those who desired it: "The important part is the option of [gender affirmation surgeries]. . . . Not every trans person is at war with their body. Not every trans person is not connected with their body. We all have varying degrees of dysphoria and certain parts we're dysphoric about." Jace, who planned to go on testosterone, as well as have top surgery, bottom surgery, and a hysterectomy, agreed with the others that surgeries are an individual choice:

> Some people don't feel like it's necessary for them and I really think it's just up to the person, like, if you feel confident in yourself and you just want people to refer to you as male pronouns, but not have any surgeries, I mean, that's really just up to you. Me and my own person, I feel like I will be overall happier and I guess like myself fulfilled if I have all these surgeries, but some people just don't think that they need it and hey, I wish I could do that, save me a lot of money.

This sentiment made sense since Jace saw himself, and other trans men, as men "trapped in female bodies." Many of the respondents who desired all of the procedures available viewed their bodies as prisons trapping them. However, no matter what they believed to be true for themselves, almost all agreed with Leo that if "they don't want surgery . . . I don't care, that's up to them, everyone has their own belief on what makes you a guy."

One problem is that the expectation of medically transitioning is still prevalent in the wider trans culture, or at least assumed to be present by the interviewees. This left many feeling judged by other trans people. It is important to note that the interviewees felt there remained a hierarchy of transness in the broader trans community, yet this large sample of trans men from the most conservative region in the country argued they did not hold these transnormative expectations. Therefore, while some trans men clearly buy into transnormative ideas, it is possible that these feelings of judgement may be based on the assumed opinions of others, rather than actual expectations of the majority of trans men. That is, it seems most trans men are more open-minded about what it means to be trans, yet they still fear the judgement of other trans men who they believe are less open-minded.

Either way, the expectation of medically transitioning—real or perceived—was detrimental to many of the men in this study. Most interviewees could not afford testosterone and surgeries, or all of the surgeries they desired, and felt other trans people deemed them as less trans because of this. Damien was infuriated by the standard of "passing" as cis in the South and the expectations of medical intervention this led to:

> It's a crock of shit that's made up. I mean 'cause let's be honest, passing is for those who want to be heteronormative. For those who wanna hold on to . . . societal gender norms that are artificial anyway. . . . It also punishes people who, like me, haven't been able to get past surgery yet. . . . It's not very fair . . . to expect that everyone should pass is some fucking norm. And what about people who are non-binary? . . . I don't like the myth of passing. . . . It's exclusionary.

He felt, at least where he lives in "the biggest small town" in Florida, passing as cis was still the standard trans men were expected to live up to. In the next chapter, I specifically examine the idea of "passing" and how passing benefits and limits trans men in the South.

Within the trans community, some refer to those who uphold this hierarchy of transness as "trans bros." Apparently, a lot of these trans bros find it entertaining to troll other trans men online. When I asked Dakota if he had experienced any prejudice or discrimination in the queer community based on his gender identity, he shared his experiences with "trans bros" online:

> "Trans bros." Have you ever heard of that? . . . trans guys, who are already on T and have their surgery and such who don't consider trans guys like myself who are pre-op and pre-T to be trans. They think they're superior and they will basically demean you until, you know, you're not trans 'cause in their eyes, you're not trans enough. . . . They basically will say like, "Oh, you know, you shouldn't be a part of this [online] group, 'cause you're not even on T yet." So, you know, you're just a girl. . . . like even like say Instagram, if you hashtag FTM, hashtag whatever, trans guys, whatever. They will go out of their way to comment on your picture and say, well you don't have facial hair, you don't look trans to me. . . . You know there's like the trans bro like the big bulked up dudes who wouldn't talk to the guys who aren't as far as in their transition, even

though you know however many years ago or whatever, they were in the same boat, they just feel more superior.

This aligns with Catalano's (2015, 417) findings that there "are widely known opinions that those who are not interested in transition options are not 'really' transgender or transsexual men," they are not "trans enough." As Catalano argues, "These messages, coming from both within and outside of the trans communities, emanate from the pervasiveness of the wrong body narrative that equates legitimacy among trans people with biomedical transitioning" (417).

The majority of the trans men I spoke with were critical of trans bros and the idea that there was one way to be trans. To me, this is a positive development within the trans community. Rubin (2003) pointed out the issue of trans bros (although they didn't refer to them that way) over fifteen years ago, and Catalano's (2015) data collected in 2012 continued to support that trans-normativity was a major issue within the trans community. Luckily, when I spoke with trans men across the Southeast in 2018, although most understood this issue, the majority no longer felt medical intervention was necessary for someone to "really" be trans. Only a few respondents held on to some of the beliefs described in Dakota's description of trans bros.

A couple of the men continued to believe that in order to be truly trans, a person had to physically transition their body to match their identity. These men felt there was a hierarchy of transness, and if you expected others to respect your gender identity, then it was your responsibility to do what it took to be legible as the gender you were trying to become. When I asked Colton if he thought it was important for trans people to have gender affirmation surgeries, he said he did:

> Yes, I mean, I kind of do. But I know there's always outliers that . . . who can't have surgery because they might be too heavy, or they might have another health condition or something. I guess it's not my place to judge who doesn't because it's not my life. I feel like, some people, I feel like I'm going to sound like a dick, but I feel like some people like expect to pass, but they don't put forth any effort to pass. And then they get upset when they get misgendered in public by people who don't know them, and they cause a big scene.

Colton understood the bias inherent in his opinion, but he admitted that he still felt like people needed to try to pass as a binary gender if they wanted to be accepted. If they didn't put forth the effort to pass, at the very least they did not have the right to get upset when people misgendered them. Frank believed that having gender affirmation surgeries was a personal preference, but agreed with Colton that if people wanted to pass then they should probably invest in surgery. Frank said, "I only believe [people need to have surgery] in so much as some people wish to pass. And just in so much that people often get misgendered or how [that makes them feel]. . . . So, I guess, I believe that they should only in so much that they don't get misgendered in public." Placing the onus on trans people to pass in order to avoid misgendering is clearly problematic. It raises questions about what it means to pass, and whose responsibility it is to label our identities.

CONCLUDING THOUGHTS

Overall, this chapter is one of the more hopeful and uplifting chapters in the book. Even in a region of the country that seems to be behind in many ways, transnormativity is beginning to recede *within* the trans community. The vast majority of the men I spoke with said there was not only one way to be trans. They respected that some people did not want to, or could not, access medical interventions, and they believed this did not make them any less trans.

While it appears transnormativity is declining, at least among trans men, most of the men continued to rely on discovery narratives to explain their own transness; whether these discovery narratives were founded in transnormativity was harder to discern. People often rely on discovery narratives to explain identities that are outside of what is expected, to themselves and to others. The continued use of discovery narratives seems to be more of a symptom of the broader society's need for those in minority groups to explain and define our "otherness." That is, this appears to be an issue of the invisibility of privilege which asks anyone who is not in the dominant group to account for their oppressed characteristics.

On the other hand, the "born in the wrong body" narratives of the men do seem to be a carryover of transnormativity related to medical gatekeepers' ability to decide if someone is "trans enough." However, while all but one of the men I spoke with had a discovery narrative tracing their identities to a younger age, only 20 continued to uphold the narrative of being born in the wrong body. With only a minority of men describing their body as wrong, and even fewer saying that being trans is a medical condition, I also see this as progress towards a less transnormative society. I am hopeful this progress will continue and that anyone who says they are trans or gender non-binary will be accepted regardless of their desire to access medical interventions.

Chapter Four

Passing in the South

Geographic location plays a key role in determining how trans men "do gender" (West and Zimmerman 1987). "Passing" denotes the ability of trans men to be seen as the gender they identify with (man, male, trans masculine, genderqueer, etc.), rather than as a woman based on the sex—female—they were assigned at birth by others (parents, medical providers, etc.) (Pfeffer 2017). The concept of passing holds negative connotations for some within academia (Pfeffer 2017; Stryker 2017) and some within the trans community (Catalano 2015). For instance, some trans men feel the concept of passing implies deceit, or that they are trying to be something they are not. Other trans men wish to pass, but are afraid of the invisibility and other issues passing can cause (Catalano 2015). Although the term "passing" is contested, it holds more potential than other concepts, such as "being recognized as" or "being read as," and it is a concept many trans people continue to identify with. Therefore, it is imperative to understand the concept of passing and its continued importance in society.

Historically, the term "passing" was first used regarding race, specifically in reference to runaway slaves. Passing signified a nonwhite person who was seen as white (Dawkins 2012); passing as white allowed runaway slaves to escape from slavery (for more on the history of passing in the U.S. see Hobbs 2014). Therefore, from its conception "passing was imbricated with strivings for freedom" (Hobbs 2014, 30). Since colonial times, passing has also been used by other minorities to gain power in an unequal and hierarchical society. Passing in this sense is not about hiding who you are, but rather being accepted for who you are and achieving your goals in an unequal society (Dawkins 2012). Consequently, to argue that "passing is passé is to presuppose that the concepts of race and racism," along with gender, sexism, transphobia, sexuality, homophobia, heteronormativity, etc., are also obsolete

(Dawkins 2012, 4; Schoenfeld 2014). The idea that passing is outdated relates to our current post-everything society—post-racist, post-feminist, post-sexist, etc. Despite the ideas of many conservatives that we live in a post-oppression society, where "diversity" and "multiculturalism" are celebrated, most Americans continue to believe in the innateness of race, gender, and sexuality and support the inequalities these beliefs uphold (Dawkins 2012; Schoenfeld 2014). In this society, where hierarchies of identities continue to prevail, passing continues to be a "way of seizing control" (Dawkins 2012, 154).

Concepts other than passing remove some of the impetus and importance behind passing. Dawkins (2012) argues that passing is the only concept that clearly demonstrates how important certain identities are to gaining privilege and access in our society. Even for those who do not desire to pass, the power and privilege that comes with passing often leads them to pass in at least some situations (Dawkins 2012). Similar to passing, "stealth" refers to trans people who choose to live privately, or not disclose their trans status to others in their public life (Reynolds and Goldstein 2014). While passing is more contextual, stealth usually refers to being seen as cis all the time in public. Some people choose to pass based on the situation or location, while those who are stealth likely never disclose their trans identities in public.

West and Zimmerman (1987; 2009) explain that everyone is held accountable to "doing gender" according to hegemonic standards of what it means to be a man or a woman in society. Doing gender in stereotypical masculine ways includes acts of domination and misogyny, and reinforces the gender binary and normative expectations of what it means to be a man. For instance, Nash (2011) finds that for trans men to be recognized as men, they must adhere to stereotypical displays of masculinity in the form of more masculine clothes, hairstyles, voice, and how they carry themselves. As Catalano (2015, 422) argues, even for trans men who wish to challenge the current gender order, "passing as a man is the only way for participants to be read as not-women, given naturalized assumptions about the gender binary (there are only men and women)."

THE IMPORTANCE OF LOCATION FOR SAFETY, FEAR, AND PSYCHOLOGICAL HEALTH

Safety and fear of violence are highly tied to geographic location. When trans men are worried about their own safety, or the safety of their families, passing allows them to curb some of that fear. As Rubin (2003, 3) explained a decade and a half ago, due to "potentially dangerous identities, many of these men prefer to be invisible." Additionally, Abelson (2014; 2019) finds that trans men's feelings of safety often determines how they do masculinities. As previously discussed, when trans men feel safer, they are more likely to practice transformative masculinities—meant to create gender equity—but when they feel threatened, they practice more defensive masculinities—more stereotypical displays of masculinity that uphold the domination of men (Abelson 2014). When trans men feel threatened, they are more likely to perform stereotypical masculinity in order to ease fear and attempt to avoid violence. As Abelson (2019, 146) explains, fear often leads trans men to adhere to "local expectations of gender and sexuality and, for white trans men, to participate at least passively in systems of racial domination when interacting in rural settings." Like others who are made to feel vulnerable in our society, trans men map out their "geographies of fear" in order to keep themselves and their families safe (Abelson 2016b; 2019). These geographies of fear are extremely important and nuanced in the South and in rural areas.

Related to safety and fear, trans men's psychological health is directly entwined with increased transphobia and homophobia in the South. Previous research demonstrates the impacts of minority stress on the life outcomes of queer people (Meyer 2003; Miller and Grollman 2015; dickey et al. 2016). It shows how stigma, prejudice, and discrimination lead to hostile and stressful environments, sometimes leading to mental health issues. Miller and Grollman (2015) examine how being visibly read as trans, what they call "stigma visibility," increases discrimination against trans people, and thereby negative health outcomes. Therefore, continued examination of trans people in the South and in rural areas is vital to improving the lives of queer people.

Overall, the South, rurality, and religion play central roles in trans men's understanding and experiences of gender, sense of safety, and desire to pass as cis men. These elements intersect to create unique experiences for trans men. As Johnson et al. (2016, 7) articulate, "Space matters where the politics of gender and sexuality in the United States are concerned, not because it is so powerfully determinative, but because its effects are so widely unpredictable." Therefore, sociologists must not only look to urban enclaves to study queer life and begin to examine queer lives in all contexts (Stone 2018).

Three primary explanations of why Southern trans men pass developed in my conversations with trans men: 1) self-confidence and psychological health; 2) the privileges of being a cis man; and 3) safety and fear of violence. While these reasons are not unique to the South, the interviewees demonstrated that these reasons are especially pronounced in this region of the country. They related the increased importance of passing to their understandings of gender and increased fear related to conservative religion, racism, and transphobia in the South. Many of the respondents understood that portraying stereotypical masculinity could be harmful to trans men, and others (women, gay men, gender non-binary people, etc.); however, most respondents felt they had no choice but to pass in this conservative region of the country.

FINDINGS: PASSING IN THE SOUTH

Despite criticism of the term "passing" in academia and the contentious nature of the term within the trans community, it continues to be largely recognized and used among the Southern trans men in this study. Avoiding the term, or calling it something different, does an injustice to the respondents who continued to identify with this concept, and ignores the continued reality and necessity of passing in an unequal and unjust society. As Stryker (2017, xi) demonstrates, "Being perceived or 'passed' as a gender-normative cisgender person grants you a kind of access to the world that is often blocked by being perceived as trans or labeled as such." It was this normative gender expression and the access to the world that it grants which most men desired. Presenting a stereotypical masculinity was related to multiple aspects of what it means to be a trans man in the South.

While some interviewees preferred the concepts of stealth, blending, or being read as men, many used these terms interchangeably with passing. Regardless of which concept they chose, across age, race, sexuality, and gender identity, the term "passing" brought up positive connotations for the majority of men in this study. Of the nine respondents who did not like the term "passing," or the fact that passing was important to them, eight still felt the need to pass. For instance, when asked what passing meant to him, Andre said, "I don't personally like that word . . . I like calling it 'being seen as you want to be seen,' because passing, to me, sounds like you're trying to trick people, to be something you're not." Nonetheless, Andre's definition of what it meant to be a man fit an extremely stereotypical definition of masculinity. Regardless of some of the respondents' feelings about the concept of "passing," all but one trans man I spoke with wanted to pass, at least in some situations. Most felt like Alec who said, "I transitioned so that I would be passable . . . I wanted to be seen as a man, not a trans man."

Similar to Alec, the desire of the interviewees to be seen as they see themselves—as men—also led other respondents to avoid being labeled as trans. Stuart, who lived in rural Tennessee, said, "I'm a guy. I'm not a trans man, I'm a legit dude, and that's just how it is. I live my lifestyle as a man, you calling me a trans man is just a label." Having lived his entire life in the South, Stuart understood the advantages of being read simply as a man, not as something "other" than. Being white and straight, along with not being viewed as trans, allowed Stuart to claim sameness in many ways and gain the privileges of being a white, straight, man.

For many respondents, passing was simple because they held a binary view of gender: if people are either men or women, and I am not a woman, then I must be a man. Jamar, who had lived the majority of his life in Tennessee, explained:

> I hate having to go by the term trans man, because the way I see it I have changed my body. . . . [and] once you have altered yourself someway . . . I don't think you should have to go by trans anymore. . . . You have gone past transitio*ning*; you have transition*ed*. . . . The act of transitioning is the phase of going from one gender to the other; that's when trans should be in your title. . . . Trans is the moving of, kind of like what transportation is . . . the vehicle used to get from one place to the other.

These trans men did not aspire to challenge the binary gender system, but rather to fit into it. Once they had reached the goal of being a man, whatever that meant to them, they wanted others to see them and address them only as men. For these respondents, transition was the time period between living life as the gender they were assigned at birth and moving to their current gender identity.

Despite some interviewees' intentions or desires to challenge the gender binary and stereotypical portrayals of masculinity, most largely upheld standards of masculinity in order to fit into the gender binary, rather than challenge or queer these standards. Trans men in the South largely attempted to blend in with cis men in their gender presentations, instead of redoing gender by doing masculinity differently. While some trans men in this study challenged stereotypical displays of masculinity in some situations, 50 of 51 interviewees consciously presented their gender in ways that conformed with stereotypical masculine presentations at least part of the time. This is not a critique of Southern trans men's gender presentations, as one trans identity or expression is not inherently more radical than another (Stryker 2017). We should not hold trans people responsible for challenging a gender system that systemically discredits their identities. This is why Stryker (2017, 5) argues that trans identities are "something prior to, or underlying, our political actions in the world and not necessarily in itself a reflection of our political beliefs." Indeed, whether they seek to challenge the gender binary or not, the act of transitioning alone can open further gender possibilities for others. At the same time, scholars *can* examine the influences of trans identities and presentations on larger systems of power and privilege. Here I examine the men's three explanations for passing in the South: 1) self-confidence and psychological health; 2) the privileges of being a cis man; 3) safety and fear of violence.

Self-Confidence & Psychological Health

For most of the interviewees (36 of 51), being read as a man was important for their self-confidence and psychological health. Being misgendered led many respondents to feel shame and self-doubt, and led to uncomfortable conversations and devaluations of their masculinity. In order to avoid awkward conversations and not be misgendered, most of the men I spoke with chose to pass. Dakota described passing as "one of the best feelings ever. . . . It is when you are in public with someone who doesn't know your background . . . and they identify you as the gender you want to be identified as, as the one, you know, you are." Again, passing is not about deception; rather it is about being seen by others and as you see yourself. Spencer explained, "I feel more comfortable in my skin when I do pass. I just feel like I'm, I don't know, it's like I'm a 100 percent there; like I'm me." To be seen in a way you do not see yourself can lead to confusion and negative psychological consequences. To be comfortable, people's identities must be validated and accepted.

Additionally, passing gives trans people the opportunity to live their lives without the constant emotional stress of explaining themselves and their bodies. For Mason, passing was most important because of how other people view trans individuals. Mason said:

> [A]s soon as someone finds out that I'm a trans man . . . it alters their perception of who I am and I'm immediately . . . emasculated. . . . So, the first question is, "Do [you] have a dick?" . . . I don't fuck around with letting people know that I'm trans or not because of how quickly it escalates to that and how I'm then just a sum of my parts, versus how I identify and who I am as a person.

Passing reduced stigma visibility and allowed trans men in the South to carry out their lives without feeling less than a man. These responses align with Rubin's (2003, 15) findings that "authenticity is a leading principle" in trans men's experiences; trans men are searching for "recognition of the innermost self" and that self is "authentically male."

Only six interviewees discussed how passing made them feel invisible in the queer community, and how this led to feelings of loneliness and isolation. This is particularly challenging when living in an area of the country where there are not a lot of other visible queer people or queer places to hang out. For illustration, Jeffrey explained, "I feel invisible now to the queer community 'cause they see me as a man, and then they see my wife as a woman, so they view us as like a heterosexual couple and it's weird." While being viewed as cis and heterosexual has many benefits, within the queer community it can make a person feel unseen and even unwanted. Similarly, Samuel felt invisible within the feminist and trans communities; he said the downside to passing was that "the isolation is awful." By being seen as a man, Samuel was ostracized from his feminist community, and being seen as cis he was ostracized from his trans community. While Samuel appreciated being seen as he sees himself, he now felt alone and cut off from the communities where he previously found support. Despite these feelings of invisibility and loneliness, the majority of trans men continued to choose passing.

In addition to changes in their relationships with the queer community, ten respondents also noticed changes in their relationships with women after they started passing as cis men. Like Nash's (2011) findings, many trans men found fitting into women's spaces difficult after transition. This is particularly detrimental considering that 29 respondents identified as lesbians before coming out as trans. One of these respondents was Donnie; he discussed how he was no longer welcomed in women's spaces after being seen as a cis man:

> Now that I'm perceived as male 100 percent of the time, there are changes in my life that . . . I just didn't necessarily anticipate the impact . . . like no longer being welcome in women's spaces . . . when you've been in that your whole life it is kind of a weird thing. Because you're like, "I'm the same person." I know rationally like why I'm not welcome in that space, but there's part of you that says, "Well, this is stupid." You know, this is another reason why gender is harmful. . . . So, it is kind of hurtful in that aspect.

When Donnie considered his experiences living as a woman prior to transition, he intellectually understood why he may no longer be welcomed in women's spaces. Emotionally, however, not being welcomed was still devastating and meant that he had to find new spaces and people to support his newly found identity. Along the same lines, Colton said, "I feel like women are more on guard around me than they were when I was just identifying as female and a lesbian." Here again we can see that some men understood how sexism and misogyny created this issue; nevertheless, they were still hurt by being excluded or viewed differently by women after their transition. Dayton put it this way: "[Women] are hearing the words through the lens of past hurts and maybe even intergenerational trauma . . . when they're talking to someone they perceive as a man; they're automatically making assumptions of hearing this oppressor talking." Especially for trans men who did not feel their personality changed due to transitioning, it was hard to reconcile their understanding of women's points of view with their desire to be accepted within the groups they were once a part of. Still, the benefits of passing continued to outweigh the disadvantages of being invisible in the queer community or treated differently by women for most of the trans men I spoke with.

Finally, regarding self-confidence and psychological health, many of the respondents mentioned body dysphoria (19 of 51) and depression (8 of 51) as key factors in their need to pass. Jace described passing as important to him because: "I do have a bunch of dysphoria about it, because I want people to take me seriously as a trans guy. . . . I don't want them to see me as just this random weird person." Similarly, Leo said, "I don't want to be seen as something I'm not at this point and it would really mess with my dysphoria. I would probably just lay in bed all day until someone told me, 'You look like a man.'" Passing as cis provided many of the men with external validation of their identity and allowed them to feel more comfortable and confident in public. For Kevin, someone referring to him using female pronouns was disrespectful and caused depression. These psychological consequences of being misgendered again point to the fact that trans people, especially those who do not pass as cis, often suffer tremendous health penalties due to transphobic discrimination and the stress this generates (Miller and Grollman 2015; dickey et al. 2016).

The Privileges of Passing

Privileges that come with being recognized as cis men were another benefit of passing. Twenty-six of 51 interviewees specifically mentioned the privileges of passing as a cis man. These privileges led some trans men to reinforce cis- and heteronormativity in order to benefit from the patriarchal dividend. These normative beliefs systems advantage cis and heterosexual people and oppress others who fall outside of these norms. By attempting to fit into these normative systems, some trans men are integrated and accepted into their communities through "claims of sameness" (Abelson 2016a), which allowed these men to find acceptance even in locations thought to be hostile to trans people. While passing for some respondents was only about being seen as they see themselves, for others it meant performing a specific type of masculinity—a type others perceive as the definition of a "man"—and gaining the privileges that accompany this performance.

Although some men cited unwanted privilege as a pitfall to passing, most also acknowledged there were benefits. The ambivalence apparent in the men's discussions of privilege exposed the difficult balance trans men must reach to be seen as they desire while simultaneously attempting not to abuse the power that comes with being a man in our society. Many trans men were granted access to gender privilege that had historically been used to oppress them; when trans men pass as cis, they have the ability to exercise this power over others.

For Leo, passing was about "making sure that I look the part, that I don't give off any . . . feminine vibes . . . making sure that my muscles are big enough . . . anything that's gonna help me fit into that masculine stereotype." Residing in suburban North Carolina at the time of his interview, Leo was able to claim sameness through identifying and presenting as a man, as well as identifying as heterosexual. However, these privileges were not absolute for Leo since now he was recognized as a *black* man. Leo said, "I'm a black male in society and so I have to be extra careful with the way I do things. I can't come off as super aggressive, I have to control my temper, you know, all that stuff." Therefore, Leo's claims to sameness were hindered by his intersecting race, which limited the privileges he could gain from passing as a man. On the contrary, Colton, who identified as a straight white male in suburban South Carolina, was able to claim sameness in terms of gender, sexuality, and race. He acknowledged how these claims of sameness worked to his benefit: "I feel like as a passing guy, actually as a passing white male, . . . I feel like I get more respect. . . . There's more of a negative connotation if you're gay in the South, than when you just pass as male."

Some of the men were worried about how the amount of privilege gained through passing as cis would change them, especially when they were both white *and* men. Jamie, who resided in an urban area in Arkansas, explained how the amount of privilege he gained as a white man in Arkansas could end up being problematic: "I am now a white male, which is probably the worst group of people for, you know, recognizing your own privilege. . . . Something I try to keep in mind is not abusing that." White men in the South must remember to stay cognizant of their privilege; otherwise, they could turn into a perpetrator of sexism and racism. Relatedly, Sage, who had lived the majority of his life in the South, but resided in an urban area in New York for school when we spoke, explained:

> I hope people never think I'm straight, I really hope I don't ever give off those vibes. . . . I don't like that I'm getting male privilege, but, I mean, I don't really have a choice in that, right? On top of white privilege, so if I'm seen as a white man, god forbid a straight white man, that's an area of privilege and access that I've never had access to. . . . As someone who often deals with cis het men, white men, I don't like them very much, I'm always guarded around them, 'cause I'm like, you're a fuck truck of privilege, like I can't trust you. And I'm very worried about entering that space myself.

Sage's recognition of privilege coupled with a desire to separate himself from it was similar to some trans men in other areas of the country. Although Sage spent most of his life in Georgia, he was living as an out queer man in urban New York when we spoke. This allowed Sage some freedom to be more open about his gender and sexuality than other trans men who were still residing in the Southeast.

For white trans men living in the South, passing provided them with privileges they were often unfamiliar with. Spencer, who resided in an urban area in Georgia, said that since passing, "I have more privilege, though I try not to abuse it . . . I notice I've gotten handshakes and more, you know, like positive interactions with other men, and like they tend to take me more seriously." Likewise, Bruno felt this change after he started passing:

> The way that men regard me is very, very different, like they listen to me more. Male privilege is very real and it's definitely interesting to step into that when I wasn't raised in it. Obviously, I knew it existed, but to see it is very strange. Men definitely . . . take [me] more seriously.

Having more positive interactions with men and being taken more seriously felt good; however, having experienced what it is like to not be taken seriously by men, some of the respondents wanted to be careful not to fall into this trap and forget where they came from. Like Spencer and Bruno, Samuel felt the difference when he began to be viewed as a cis man:

> [Passing] gives me more of a seat at the table than I've ever had before. . . . I just feel like I'm taken more seriously, and that could probably also be like male privilege stuff, I'm sure. Uh, although I feel like very complicated about my place in that just because as soon as someone finds out I'm trans, they kind of pull the rug out from under me a lot of times.

Spencer, Bruno, and Samuel had all three lived their entire lives in the South and represented the three various types of locations—urban, rural, and suburban. Each said they found privilege when passing as cis men in the South, and each of them identified as white. They all used the phrase that after passing they were "taken more seriously" by other men. While these positive interactions and privileges were found across the region for white men, who could claim sameness in terms of race and gender, they all also understood that there was always the possibility of being "found out" and these privileges disappear. These men presumed these privileges were revocable and in order to keep them they must continue to be viewed as men, and not as trans. If you want a seat at the table and your voice heard and taken seriously you must continue to pass. This is the tragedy of passing, "that some passers see passing as the only path to social equality," and they are likely correct in certain contexts and locations (Dawkins 2012, 155–156).

Unmistakably, passing as a black man did not convey the same privileges as passing as a white man in the South. Three of the six black men specifically mentioned the disadvantages that come with passing as a black man. In addition to Leo, whom I discussed earlier, Andre, a black trans man from urban Georgia, said, "I do realize what it means to be a black man in America. . . . It means, walking in an elevator and . . . an old white lady clutching her purse, like, oh my gosh, like it's a black man with me." Likewise, Ronald acknowledged his male privilege, but explained that this privilege was often countered by his race: "[B]eing a black man is a disadvantage. Now people are afraid of me. I'm not a scary guy, but people are afraid." Future research needs to examine more closely how race and class intersect with trans identities and passing regarding privilege, as well as safety and fear.

Another important intersecting characteristic related to privilege was sexuality. While trans men in other areas of the country often do not wish to pass as cis and/or heterosexual men (Catalano 2015; Rowniak and Chesla 2013), a sizable proportion of the men I spoke with in the South preferred to pass as both of these. Thirty of the 51 men identified their gender as male (not trans male) and 18 identified their sexuality as straight. Heterosexuality allowed some trans men to more closely align with hegemonically masculine ideals (R. Connell and Messerschmidt 2005) through compensatory manhood acts (Schrock and Schwalbe 2009). That is, by performing a stereotypical cis heterosexual masculinity, some trans men in this study gained the benefits that come with being a man in our society. Overall, unlike the respondents in other studies (Sumerau et al. 2018), the majority of heterosexual trans men in this study did not reject cisnormative definitions of gender, nor articulate more gender-expansive interpretations of heterosexuality. Many of the trans men in this study differed from trans people in other studies who were more likely to identify outside of the gender binary and as bi+ (Catalano 2015; Galupo et al. 2014; Flores et al. 2016; Rowniak and Chesla 2013; Sumerau et al. 2018). Trans men in the South often adhered to hegemonic understandings of masculinity—tied to compulsive heterosexuality, as heterosexuality is an important component to passing in the South—in order to pass as cis men. While some respondents indicated that cis assumptions did not align with their experiences, the majority of those who identified as heterosexual did not "disrupt societal assumptions about the necessity of cisnormativity for heterosexual selves" (Sumerau et al. 2018, 8). These men desired to be read as cis and assume the privileges that come along with being men, especially the ability to attract and protect women.

For other men, their desire to pass as cis went against their understanding of gender and aspiration to be activists for the trans community. However, even these men, who held a more nuanced understanding of gender, still found passing to be an important element of transition. Some recognized this incongruence, yet for various reasons felt that the need to pass outweighed their need to challenge the gender binary. For instance, when I asked Sage if it was important for him to pass, he said,

> So, the good little activist inside me is like, "No! Fuck passing! I'm gonna be . . . whatever the hell I want!" . . . But, um, I really do want to pass, just for safety,

for my sake of mind, it feels good, it feels consistent, and it doesn't feel good to be misgendered.

I asked Sage if he felt differently about passing in the South, versus where he lived in New York at the time of the interview. He said,

In the South, I could pretty much only be out in my community, with my friends. If someone at a restaurant or other things misgendered me, I just wouldn't say anything, I always went the kind of polite, high-pitched public service voice of like, [pitches voice] "Oh, thank you, okay." Very much on that side of caution . . . I felt there was an additional layer of either bravado or safety.

Likewise, Samuel told me that trans was an important part of his identity: "I'm not a cis guy and I don't want to be a cis guy"; however, he explained, "I guess [passing] is important to me, contrary to all the other shit I've said. It is still really important to me 'cause I just know I wouldn't handle it well if all of the sudden, I wasn't passing." When I asked Samuel if he thought his need to pass was related to living in the South, he said he would need to pass no matter where he lived for mental health reasons, but went on to say, "I tell you the Southeast is probably about as bad as it gets in America to be a trans person."

Safety & Fear

One reason the Southeast is "as bad as it gets" is due to safety and fear of violence in the region. In total, 28 of 51 interviewees mentioned safety and fear as reasons they desired to pass. Safety and fear are consistent themes across research on trans men's desire to pass. Like trans men in other studies (Abelson 2016b; 2019), the men in this study mapped out their fears to specific locations and geographic areas. While perceptions of fear did not necessarily align with actual violence in the areas, the South and rural areas led trans men to fear violence. This is especially problematic because, whether the respondents faced actual transphobic violence or discrimination, fear changed how trans men lived their lives and led them to participate in other oppressive systems in order to be accepted and, for most, to continue to pass as cis men.

While expectations of Southern masculinity were related to respondents' self-confidence, psychological health, and the privileges of being recognized as cis men, their feelings of safety and fear provoked the most ardent desire to pass. Hugh put it this way:

A few years ago, I was more open about my gender identity . . . but since I've gotten further in my transition . . . I'm a little more stealth than I used to be. . . .

I don't really like that [passing] is so important to me, but when I feel like I don't pass, it really, it's hard. . . . If I was living in a different area of the country, I feel like I would be able to more openly express my trans identity, without as much fear and repercussions.

When I asked respondents if the South had any influence on their desire to pass, a large proportion directly tied their feelings of safety and fear to conservative religion, rurality, and racism. Gordon had spent more years in the South than any other respondent in this study—37 years to be exact. When we spoke, Gordon lived in rural Georgia and fully felt the impact of geographic location on his trans identity. Gordon said living in the South impacts his need to pass because "we're in the heart of the Bible Belt. . . . People are still very close-minded. . . . And people fear what they don't understand." He tied his feelings about the South directly to conservative religion and other fear of difference, both of which could provoke hatred or violence.

Bruno agreed that the South has "a very different mentality . . . there's a lot more bigotry here because religion is really deeply tied to the way of life here. . . . I definitely have gone out of my way to not be visibly trans or visibly queer." In rural South Carolina, Bruno believed that passing protected him from people who tied their hatred of trans people to their religious beliefs. Similarly, Stuart demonstrated the fear caused by living in the rural South: "[Y]ou'll get killed down here. There'll be some redneck honky people that would just kill you in a parking lot . . . just because you're trans. . . . Because they think . . . you're going against what God made you." Rurality and religion were closely tied realities that occupied the nightmares of trans men in the South. Although most fears of religion were tied to rurality, Jamar, who lives in suburban Tennessee, also felt religion influenced his fear of living in the South as a trans man:

Being in the South . . . I have nothing against Christianity, but the way it is taught here, it is, you were meant to be the way the Bible says . . . so [trans people] fear a lot of times for our own very lives at times, because of that upbringing and that religious belief. . . . Closed-minded Christians are the deadliest of all the Christians; they are the ones that go out and will beat the shit out of somebody.

As these quotes demonstrate, it was largely due to conservative religion that many trans individuals felt that living in the South forced them to hide their trans identity.

While many respondents linked their need to pass to religion, others directly related it to symbols of racism and bigotry. Thirteen of 51 respondents discussed racism, such as the Klu Klux Klan and the confederate/rebel flag, as evidence of why they needed to be careful to pass as cis men. Interestingly, all but one of the thirteen men who discussed racism identified as white. The visibility of racism in the South was used by many white trans men as a proxy for transphobia and general bigotry. Abelson (2019, 34) also found the trans men she spoke to "entwined the redneck with racism, homophobia, sexism, and violence, and the redneck was placed in rural spaces. . . . This is why trans men viewed rural spaces as particularly unsafe for anyone who was not like the redneck." For instance, Darius, a 23-year-old white asexual male who lived in urban Georgia, explained: "[T]his is such a red state . . . Southeastern state that . . . the fear is there. You can still drive by porches and see confederate flags, and that always, you know, is dangerous . . . I have to remember that like the danger is real." Darius, like other men in this study, used any sign of bigotry as a symbol to remember that they could be unsafe in the area.

Because signs of bigotry are often more overt in the rural South, many assume that trans people would either prefer the city or move out of the Southeast. On the contrary, trans men were able to use these signs of bigotry to determine what areas were safe and what areas were dangerous. While it may seem paradoxical, overt symbols of bigotry allow queer people to navigate spaces and map their geographies of fear more precisely than in other areas of the country where signs of racism, homophobia, and transphobia are less overt. Nolan, who had lived his entire life in the South, said:

> [T]he South is definitely not the safest place in the world to be trans. There's a whole lot of backwoods mindset and I have come to find that anytime you are in an area that is racist, you are also in an area that's genderist, that will not understand it. And sadly, the South has definitely got a higher concentration of that.

By looking for signs of overt racism, trans people can pinpoint areas that are less accepting and avoid those areas to keep themselves safe.

The fear induced by living in the South as a queer person was mitigated, at least to a degree, by passing. For Trip, in suburban Georgia passing was important because "if you don't fit in, you're in trouble . . . nothing feels safe in the South." By fitting in, things start to feel safer. Likewise, according to Rowen, who had lived his entire life in the South:

> Before I was passing . . . I would be afraid to be with my fiancé, because we lived in such a close-minded place and deep in the South . . . I was always afraid that somebody would say something or confront us or in the worst cases, try to hurt us, and honestly, I haven't felt that since I started passing a lot more.

When other people see you as one of them (in this case white, straight, and a man), fears dissipate and trans men feel more comfortable in public. Rowen feared that he would not only be hurt if people knew he was trans, but also that he was putting his family at risk. Similarly, Jorge, who lived in suburban Georgia, feared for himself and his family. He passed to keep his family safe: "I hide the fact that I'm trans, usually. . . . It's important for me to be just like any other regular guy . . . you have a wife and child, it's like you can't go blasting that you're trans everywhere, because you've got to keep your family safe."

Garrett also spent his entire life in the South and summed up why living in the South was an important component to understanding the intersections of geographic location and gender identity:

> Living in the South is a very scary thing . . . I make more of an effort [to pass] . . . I used to be pretty open about my transness . . . but like, this whole overwhelming anxiety about living in the South, in a highly conservative area, has me like constantly looking at my surroundings and counting exits and hating big crowds, refusing to go to the bathroom.

Garrett, who was a college student in Georgia when we spoke, explained that while he was in high school he had urinary tract infections because he was afraid to go to the bathroom. He said as a result he would sometimes pass out from not drinking enough water. For him, there "was just like an overwhelming fear about it." Jamar said that where he lived in Tennessee, "to not pass could be dangerous. There are certain parts of [the city] that if you don't pass, and you go to the bathroom, they will corner you and beat the shit out of you." In fact, the bathroom was so important that Jamie defined passing simply as "being able to go to the bathroom and pee." These fears led the men to present a more cis-masculine and heteronormative presentation of gender.

Just as some men's fears revolved around bathrooms, other trans men in the South provided exact locations and precise maps of where they felt safe and where they felt unsafe. Jayden had lived his entire life in the South and resided in urban Virginia at the time of his interview; he explained that in the South, "anybody that has the non-passability issue or is struggling with passability is 100 percent always, always, concerned for their safety." When I asked if there were certain situations or places where he felt the need to pass was greater, he said:

> [O]ne of the biggest situations where I want to make sure I'm 100 percent passable, is a country [music] concert. You're going to have a lot of country guys, there's going to be a lot of drinking involved, there's going to be a lot of masculinity involved . . . and if you're not on their level . . . sometimes you become part of an issue, and when you're in a big venue like that . . . blending in is key.

Respondents recognized that they did not want to stand out in a crowd, especially in spaces marked as country or rural. Places marked as country or rural were likely to have rednecks in them and rednecks by definition are hypermasculine and dangerous.

Alec lived his whole life in the South and resided in an urban area in Tennessee when we talked. He gave the example of a flea market as a location where passing was necessary in the rural South. Alec explained, "A lot of people that come to the flea market are from small towns and country bumpkins. . . . I do not want them knowing I'm transgender, because Bubba over there might be a real asshole and want to beat my ass in the bathroom." Again, the redneck and the restroom played prominent roles in Southern trans men's geographies of fear. This aligns with Abelson's (2019) findings of trans men across the country, although the specifics of Bubba in the bathroom demonstrate the particularly Southern and rural elements of these fears. Though trans men rarely face violence in restrooms, especially men's restrooms, the fear is genuine and influences the way trans men move through space and their everyday lives (Abelson 2019).

Darius described living in the South as "scary for a trans person." He said, "I'm kind of lucky 'cause I'm a white guy, so it's a little less scary . . . but there is a lingering fear of like the average age a trans person lives to is in their 30s." Some of these fears were based in ideology, not facts; nevertheless, they had an extreme influence on the lives of the trans men I spoke with. While research does not confirm Darius' belief that trans people's life expectancy is in their 30s, this number had a huge influence on Darius's life. A number often cited, but not established by research, is that the average life expectancy of trans women of color is 35 years. Darius, a white person who identified as a man in urban Georgia, was likely safe from transphobic violence, but his fear of extreme violence, or murder, most definitely influenced his quality of life.

Living in the South limits the options of gender expression for some trans men and the locations they inhabit in their everyday lives. Research that suggests gender is being undone (Deutsch 2007), or that masculinities are now inclusive and no longer homophobic (Anderson 2016), is clearly not being conducted in the Southeast. Yet, despite trans men's magnified fears in the South, many chose to stay and carry out their lives in Southern and rural areas. Many of these men identified strongly with Southern and/or rural culture and chose to stay despite some of the obvious downfalls. Several of the respondents indicated they would have felt out of place, or even more unsafe, in larger cities due to their Southern and rural cultures.

CONCLUDING THOUGHTS

Trans men in the Southeast desire to pass, whether they like it or not. The vast majority of trans men in this study "do gender" through passing and enacting hegemonic ideals of masculinity. While some of the respondents held more nuanced views of gender, and some wished to challenge the gender binary system, their need or desire to pass usually outweighed their desire to challenge gender norms. Nevertheless, these men's experiences of gender are extremely important for thinking about gender. As Dawkins (2012, 156) demonstrates, listening to the stories of people who are passing allows us to learn more about inequality and to empower the passers in some ways:

> Passers tell stories that show us how we all are duped as society's injustices are concealed and revealed in an attempt to embody democratic and progressive ideals. . . . If society stops passing, as moral, just, free, or equal, for instance, then the need many potential passers express for projecting more "acceptable" personae and "valuable" identities would end. . . . When passers identify themselves sincerely, they can reveal society's injustices and inequalities. . . . Failing to acknowledge things said in passing also means that all passers are destined to remain prisoners in solitary confinement because society says they have committed some crime of identity theft. (156)

Overall, we must listen to those who desire to pass. We must hear their stories and use their language to demonstrate the continued limits of a binary gender system, or any binary system, for that matter. Trans men who pass allow us to see the social construction of both sex and gender. Additionally, trans men clearly demonstrate the privileges that men continue to receive over women, and other trans and gender non-binary people who cannot or do not pass. By choosing to ignore, or reframe, trans men's desire to pass, we give power to the idea that "passing is passé" and this stops us short of fighting for a society where nothing is seen as passing, or everything is seen as passing; a society where we can all just be ourselves.

Passing is highly related to the geographic location of the South, which in many ways remains a location that is less free and less just than other areas of the country—or at least perceived that way. In an area of the U.S. known for increased transphobia, homophobia, and biphobia, trans men feel an amplified need to pass. Trans men's desire to pass is related to self-confidence and psychological health; the privileges of being a cis man; and safety and fear of violence. While the benefits of passing outweigh the disadvantages, some trans men do point to problems with passing, such as changes in relationships with women, issues of invisibility within the queer community, and for nonwhite men, the consequences of being a man of color in the U.S. These advantages and disadvantages of passing could be overcome if people could present themselves in the way they felt most comfortable, without fear of reprisal. Passing could become passé in regard to gender, but only when people receive equal benefits and privileges regardless of gender. If we acknowledge that we are all passing, that gender and other identities we hold are not innate, but are socially constructed in an unequal and hierarchical system, then we could end the negativity around passing and all pass as ourselves.

Overall, trans men pass in order to protect their well-being and gain privileges. Again, trans men's attempts to pass should be viewed as part of the flawed binary social structure of gender, not a shortcoming of trans men (Pfeffer 2017). It should be viewed as a demonstration of inequality and a call for justice rather than an individual act of deception. As Dawkins (2012, 157–158) concludes:

> Our desperation to declare that we have progressed beyond passing, simply because we fail to acknowledge passers and the things they say, means that we continue to cultivate an environment in which passing will remain the most sincere strategy for success. The unfortunate result of this problem is a form of cultural neglect through which we abandon opportunities to engage in the important work of reconciliation that can lead to social change. We fail to see that every act of passing presents an opportunity for reconciliation, expresses a desire for social change, and calls for the freedom to be who we are.

Trans men's desire to pass is a call for everyone to engage in the undoing of a limiting and unequal binary gender system. It is a call for justice and a demonstration of the oppression trans men face in our society.

Passing demonstrates the importance of geographic location, the South, rural areas, and the "ordinary cities" (Johnson et al. 2016; Stone 2018) when considering trans men. By further nuancing our understanding of trans men in the South, we can expand understandings of gender, masculinity, and passing. The South remains a location with elevated minority stressors, where fitting into the gender binary through passing and engaging in compensatory manhood acts (Schrock and Schwalbe 2009) makes life more livable for many trans men. Through claims of sameness trans men can carry out their lives in the South in a relatively privileged and safe way. This may explain why many trans men opt to stay in the South, even when options to leave are available. Like some rural lesbians (Kazyak 2012), trans men's presentation of masculinity and rurality make them more comfortable in the South and rural areas, despite the downfalls of conservative religion, racism, and toxic masculinity.

Scholars proposing an inclusive form of masculinity (Anderson 2016) have failed to consider geographic location an important intersecting characteristic in their work. Inclusive masculinity is not a reality in the South if it is in any region. In this region of the country, masculinity remains largely tied to heterosexuality, stereotypical manhood acts, and privilege and inequality. Even when "doing transgender," many trans men in the South do not develop a "feminist consciousness" (C. Connell 2010), largely due to the constraints placed on the "proper" presentation of masculinity in this area of the country. My findings more closely align with some of Schilt's (2006) respondents who did not gain a feminist consciousness from passing as men. As Schilt (2006, 474) puts it, "Having a critical perspective on gender discrimination . . . is not inherent" to trans men's experiences. Negative characteristics of Southern masculinity related to aggression, treatment of women, and homophobia mean that many trans men must decide between being accepted as "one of the boys," or a feminist consciousness that allows them to develop a masculinity not based on the oppression of others. As Schilt and C. Connell (2007) explain, those around trans men may play a large role in forcing trans men to "do gender," rather than "cause gender trouble." That is, in order to fit in, get privileges, and not disrupt systems, many trans men choose, or are forced, to present gender in stereotypical ways. Of course, these expectations also vary based on other intersecting characteristics, such as race, class, or sexuality.

Future research should continue to examine the intersecting characteristics that negate the benefits of passing in the South. For instance, we know that race plays a vital role in the type of experiences trans men encounter (Abelson 2019; Halberstam 2018), especially in the South, and in rural areas, where there are unique histories of racial oppression. Unfortunately, the majority of research on trans men to this point lacks the racial diversity necessary to fully understand the impacts of race on trans identities. Research on trans and non-binary identities must continue to reach out to racially diverse communities. This will require scholars to engage in new strategies for recruiting participants, ensure the use of inclusive and diverse language, and work with more scholars of color who know and are a part of these communities. In addition to race, trans research should also examine what other intersecting characteristics—such as class, ability, sexuality, ethnicity, immigration status—influence trans men's desire to pass, and lives more generally. Finally, more research is needed to understand non-binary identities in the South. How do those who do not desire to pass differ from the trans men in this study? Overall, these advances in research will require more diversity in our samples and culturally competent scholars who are willing to work with and listen to trans and non-binary people.

Chapter Five

Losing My Religion

The Bible Belt consists of three census regions: South Atlantic (West Virginia, Virginia, Maryland, Delaware, North Carolina, South Carolina, Georgia, and Florida), East South Central (Kentucky, Tennessee, Mississippi, and Alabama), and West South Central (Texas, Oklahoma, Arkansas, and Louisiana) (Barton 2012). These regions overlap with the Southeastern United States where all of the respondents in this study have lived. Overall, the Bible Belt is a region where "Protestant Christianity overshadows other forms of religious expression" (Barton 2012, 9). Barton explains that Bible Belt Christianity is not limited only to churches or Sundays. In fact, they argue, even for those who do not identify as Christian,

> this particular brand of Christianity permeates the multiple environments in which residents work, socialize, and worship. Christian crosses, messages, paraphernalia, music, news, and attitudes saturate everyday settings. Bible Belt Christianity thus influences a wide range of local secular institutions like schools and workplaces, and Bible Belt Christians exert a powerful influence on city, county, and state political and cultural institutions. (14)

Additionally, Sumerau and Cragun (2018, xxii) contend that often gender and sexuality play a more important role in determining who is accepted in a religious or spiritual community than religious and spiritual beliefs and practices themselves: "Gender and sexual norms and requirements often outweigh spirituality and religious practice in determining who counts as members of a given religion in many cases." Due to Bible Belt Christianity, the Southeast is a "region where research would suggest people are more likely to, despite shifting national patterns, explicitly condemn sexual and gender diversity when given the chance to speak freely" (Sumerau, Grollman, and Cragun 2018, 7).

Barton's analysis clearly shows that "the vast majority of places one might worship in the Bible Belt are homophobic" (13). Even as some Christian institutions in the Bible Belt become less homophobic and begin to view some cis lesbian women and gay men as "potentially moral," transphobia remains a vital aspect of separating Christians from the general population, especially in the South (Mathers, Sumerau, and Cragun 2018; Sumerau and Cragun 2018; Sumerau, Grollman, and Cragun 2018, 4). Cis lesbian women and cis gay men are gaining acceptance in some Christian churches by adhering to essentialist views of gender, sexuality, and family. As Sumerau and Cragun (2018, ix) put it:

> Lesbian and gay conformity to monogamous marriage, biologically determined monosexuality, cisgender self-presentations, and academic/religious theories about sex and gender, whiteness, middle-class respectability, nuclear family formation, and religious participation may have limited to no benefits for bisexual, transgender, poly, and/or nonreligious people (BTPN) in America.

Similarly, in an analysis of lesbian- and gay-affirming congregations, McQueeney (2009, 170) explains, "By essentializing sexuality and defining its expression as proper only in two forms—hetero- or homosexual monogamy—members made the churches less inclusive of bisexuals, transgender people, and gender and sexual nonconformists who seek freedom from sexual roles and hierarchies" (see also Sumerau 2012). Overall, research demonstrates that "cisnormativity is built into dominant notions of what it means to be a Christian in contemporary America" (Sumerau and Cragun 2018, 20).

The Pew Research Center (2014) estimates that 76 percent of people in the South identify as Christian, compared to 65 percent in the Northeast and 64 percent in the West. Of those Christians in the region, the majority (59 percent) identify as Protestant, with 34 percent identifying as evangelical, 14 percent as mainline, and 11 percent identifying with a historically black church (Pew Research Center 2014). Additionally, 15 percent of people in the South identify as Catholic. The South remains a predominately Christian region. How then do trans men navigate this highly religious area of the country? Are trans men in the Bible Belt able to reconcile the religion they were raised in with their trans identities?

In this chapter, I present an exploratory analysis of trans men's religious and spiritual beliefs and identities. While research concerning Christians' beliefs and attitudes toward queer people, especially cis gay men and cis lesbian women, has proliferated over the last few decades (Altemeyer and Hunsberger 1992; Baker and Brauner-Otto 2015; Cragun and Sumerau 2015; Duck and Hunsberger 1999; Rowatt et al. 2006; Sumerau, Grollman, and Cragun 2018), little research has examined trans people's views about religion and spirituality. I define religion as "a set of beliefs and practices focused on the sacred or supernatural, through which life experiences of groups and individuals are given meaning and direction" (Emerson and Smith 2000, 17). Previous studies have largely ignored religions outside of Christianity and ignored spirituality altogether (Cragun and Sumerau 2015). Further, Cragun and Sumerau (2015, 821) point out that based on current research "[i]t is unclear whether shifting attitudes concerning lesbian and gay people trigger similar shifts in opinions regarding bisexual, transgender, or other marginalized communities," and find in their most recent book on the topic, *Christianity and the Limits of Minority Acceptance in America* (Sumerau and Cragun 2018), that they do not.

My goal is to provide a starting point for understanding trans men's religious identities and beliefs by showing how trans men's identities and beliefs shift over their lives. I continue the process that Sumerau and Cragun (2018, xiv–xv) began, to move scholarship "beyond cisnormative, mononormative, and . . . religionormative foci." In a culture characterized by religionormativity—"efforts to enforce religion and religious norms on individuals"—I examine how trans men navigate these norms, specifically in the Southeast where they are omnipresent and often feel inescapable. I assess religion through the lens of trans people, rather than how others view trans people within religion. I want to understand if, and how, trans people continue to hold religious and spiritual beliefs despite how religion often frames them. As Sumerau and Cragun (2018, xix) explain, "People define themselves as real men and women in a world with other real women and men by defining transgender and intersex people as unnatural and absent from god's creation or their science's understanding of the natural world." How do trans men in the South understand their religious and spiritual beliefs in light of being framed as "unnatural and absent from god's creation"?

FINDINGS: SOUTHERN TRANS MEN'S RELIGIOUS & SPIRITUAL EXPERIENCES AND BELIEFS

Overall, 45 of the 51 trans men in this study were raised in a Christian church. Most were raised evangelical Protestant, including Baptist, Southern Baptist, Non-Denominational, Pentecostal, and Church of Christ. Only four interviewees had no religious background and two were raised Pagan. However, at the time of the interviews only 13 respondents continued to identify as Christian, and none of the interviewees continued to identify as evangelical Protestant or Catholic. Moreover, only four respondents identified with a specific denomination, all within mainline Protestantism—specifically, Methodist or Episcopalian. In addition to the 25 percent of trans men who identified as Christians, three interviewees identified as Pagan, one as Pantheist, and one with Indigenous spirituality.

Table 5.1. Religious and Spiritual Identities

Religious/Spiritual Identity	Respondents
Agnostic	Tobias
Atheist	Donnie; Jeffrey; Reece; Zac
Christian	Dakota; Emmett; Jamie; Javier; Leo; Quentin; Vincent
Christian - Methodist/ Episcopal	Frank; Lamar; Stuart; Timothy
Christian/Indigenous Spirituality	Mason
Christian/Pagan	Jorge
None	Carter; Derek; Eli; Garrett; Hugh; Jace; Kevin; Maddox; Max; Parker; Ronald; Rowen; Theo
Pagan	Devin; Jamar
Pantheist	Bruno
Spiritual, Not Religious	Alec; Andre; Billy; Colton; Darius; Dayton; Gabriel; Gordon; Hayden; Jayden; Liam; Nolan; Sage; Samuel; Spencer; Trip; Walker

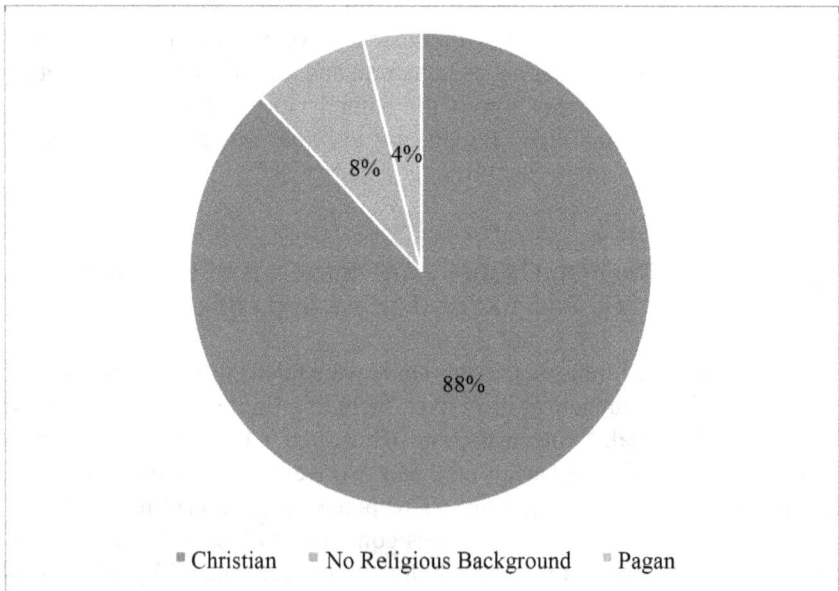

■ Christian   ■ No Religious Background   ■ Pagan

Raised Religious Identity

Research shows that younger people in the U.S. are becoming less religious (Kosmin, Keysar, Cragun, and Navarro-Rivera 2009). Many young people appear to be leaving religions due to homophobic and transphobic teachings these religions support (Jones, Cox, and Navarro-Rivera 2014). For trans men, this trend of leaving religion may be more universal, and not solely based on age—which did not correlate with religious and spiritual beliefs in this study. In their book on trans Christians, Hartke (2018) explains, "Trans Christians face incredible obstacles in churches around the world. While some of us find ways to make it back into affirming communities with a faith that's still strong, not all of us have found that fountain of healing yet." Furthermore, Adler (2012) suggests homophobia and transphobia within Christianity, in particular, will linger due to the changing demographics of the Christian church in the United States. With a decreasing share of white mainline Protestants, and the majority of those who attend religious services becoming older and more conservative, progressive change will be gradual within the church (Adler 2012). The recent decision by the United Methodist Church (UMC) General Conference in 2019 to uphold the "Traditional Plan"—one which prohibits same-sex marriages and ordination of lesbian and gay clergy members in the church—appears to align with Adler's predictions. For a mainline Protestant denomination in 2019 to uphold a plan that essentially tells "self-avowed practicing homosexuals" to see themselves out of the UMC, it is not surprising that many trans men felt the need to leave their religions.

LOSING AND LEAVING MY RELIGION

Due to homophobic and transphobic beliefs, many trans men in the Bible Belt chose to separate themselves from religion. Jace provided details about the specific experience that led him to leave his Southern Baptist church in Georgia. When Jace began his gender transition, the pastor publicly reprimanded him in a sermon. He explained:

> The first month that I came out [as trans] and it got around church . . . [the pastor's] sermon was "What's Wrong with You and Why You Need Jesus." Yeah, that was the actual name of the sermon. He started into this, "If you feel like you are not in the right body, then you need Jesus because Jesus put you in that body for a reason and you need to keep that body sacred and what you're doing is just wrong." He just kind of looked at me and directed it towards me and then everybody else kind of looked and then he started into, "Once you desecrate your body like that, you're going to Hell."

After this experience, Jace no longer felt comfortable in his church and decided he didn't need it. Similarly, Jayden was attending a Southern Baptist church when he came out as lesbian (before coming out as trans). He described being very involved in his youth group until the other members of the group began to shun him. Jayden said his "beliefs were wavered and deterred because of people, not because of the belief." Jayden was forced to leave his religion and was left with nowhere to practice his beliefs.

Another interviewee, Rowen, also grew up in a Southern Baptist church in the South and described how his church "always kind of lumped homosexual and transgender in the same category as murderers and rapists." Eventually, Rowen separated himself from this toxic environment and said he hasn't "really found God again since then." Homophobia and transphobia forced these Southern Baptists to leave their religion, which made it clear they were not worthy or welcome in their congregations. Using homophobia, transphobia, and cis- and heteronormativity, many religions, especially evangelical Protestantism, "others" gender and sexual minorities. In order to protect their identity, what Smith et al. (1998) refer to as subcultural identity, evangelical Protestants place certain groups outside of the bounds of acceptable living (Rogers 2019b). The way this is often done "is by the creation and dissemination of statements that this or that group, practice, or appearance is sinful or immoral in the eyes of God" (Sumerau and Cragun 2018, 21).

Several of the trans men who left their religion felt a desire to find their spiritual beliefs again, but due to their experiences with religion in the South, many found this difficult, if not impossible. Trip discussed his desire to find spirituality again despite the disconnect he felt with religion and spirituality caused by the homophobia and transphobia in the church: "I think [religion and spirituality are] more important than I want to let on. I have existential crises every month or so, but that didn't used to happen when I was heavily religious. But, it's hard for me to believe in things that I was taught . . . and then seeing how my family acted towards me [when I came out]. It's just, something's disconnected." Trip, like many queer religious people, found meaning in religion and spirituality, but after witnessing its negative effects could not figure out a way to reconcile the two. Billy, who lived almost his entire life in the South, had a similar experience. He described being raised Christian and "for a little while, I identified as queer and Christian." Then, he went to Liberty University, a Christian university in Virginia, which was marketed to him as an accepting environment for gender and sexual minorities; he found that this was not the case. Billy said every class, sermon, and conversation revolved around "underhanded gay bashing." After this experience, Billy said he no longer identified as religious.

For these trans men, the cognitive dissonance—psychological discomfort caused by facing two conflicting realities (Festinger 1957; Mahaffy 1996)—between religion, especially evangelical Protestantism, and identifying as trans was too great. According to Mahaffy (1996), cognitive dissonance can be dealt with in three ways: 1) altering one's religious beliefs, 2) leaving the church, or 3) living with the psychological discomfort. Cragun and Sumerau (2015, 830) explain that many people who leave religion "may retain certain elements of religion—elements that can be divorced from institutional religion, that they find beneficial, such as believing all humans are connected or there is a higher power or purpose for existence." My findings support this; many people are leaving religion yet maintaining their religious and spiritual beliefs. This chapter also expands research by specifically looking at this trend within a gender minority community.

Many of the trans men left their religion, but maintained spiritual beliefs. Alec explained, "Religion can poison people's mind, but spirituality is just more about you and your maker and an understanding between the two of you that no one else has anything to do with." Relatedly, Bruno said:

I think spirituality is innate to us, and that's great, but I think religion was very much created, if that makes sense. I think that religion lost its way somewhere along the line, so . . . religion's not necessarily my thing. [Spirituality] is extremely important because I think that spirituality is just one of the cornerstones of taking care of yourself. You know, you have to have something to believe in and something that brings you peace, whatever that is, and I think that spirituality is that for a lot of people.

Many respondents felt that the word "religion" itself had become toxic. For example, Nolan explained, "I'm not a Bible thumper and so I hate to use the term religious because it just has so many negative connotations with something it's not." Along the same lines, Dayton expounded, "I feel inspired by a number of religions and I feel like I have a connection with God, or I usually use the word 'source'. . . the word 'religion' to me feels restrictive." Finally, Gordon said that although he has faith in God, the word "religion" to him is "very confining."

Research refers to this group of individuals who leave religion, but not necessarily spiritual beliefs, as "Nones" (Kosmin et al. 2009). As Kosmin et al. (2009, i) explain, "'None' is not a movement, but a label for a diverse group of people who do not identify with any of the myriad of religious options in the American religious marketplace. . . . Some believe in God; some do not. Some may participate occasionally in religious rituals; others never will . . . only a small minority are atheists." According to the Pew Research Center (2014), approximately 23 percent of people in the United States identify as

"Nones," with only 3 percent of those identifying as Atheists. In the South, which includes all of the states in this study, the percentage of "Nones" is around 19 percent (Pew Research Center 2014). Conversely, the majority (34 of 51) of trans men in this study fit into the "None" category—which includes one Agnostic respondent, four Atheist respondents, thirteen respondents who identified with no religion, and sixteen respondents who identified as spiritual but not religious.

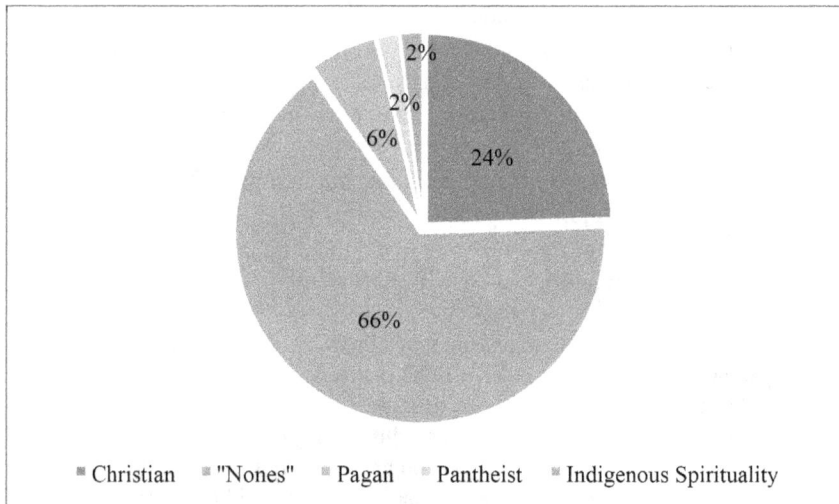

Religious Identity

Even those respondents who remained religious or spiritual admitted that practicing religion and spirituality was difficult for them. Dakota continued to identify as Christian, but said he no longer attended a church due to the homophobia and transphobia he experienced: "I don't believe that my God is a hateful God. I don't believe that He says, 'Oh, well, you're homosexual. You're going to Hell.' I feel like He's a very loving God and that people are portraying Him to be something He's not. . . . Going to church doesn't make me any more of a Christian than standing in a garage makes me a car." While Dakota did not separate himself from his religion, he did remove himself from the religious institution. He clarified, "I don't feel the need to go to that institution to believe and to pray and praise and whatnot. I can do that from the comforts of my own home." Sage explained, "I veer more towards spirituality or mindfulness or just being present. I do think there's something bigger out there or a greater universal force, but lord knows I have enough to deal with right now on the corporeal plane." Like Sage, several other respondents felt they had more important or pressing issues to deal with than their religious or spiritual beliefs, or the religious institutions that shunned them.

RACE AND RELIGION

When considering trans men's religious identities and beliefs, the importance of the intersections of race cannot be overlooked. In the United States, race continues to play an important role in determining religious beliefs. In *Divided by Faith: Evangelical Religion and the Problem of Race in America*, Emerson and Smith trace the intersections of race and religion, specifically within evangelical Protestantism, from the early 1700s to present day (or at least to the year 2000 when the book was published). They note that "it is ironic that as racial thinking became more egalitarian, and as laws were passed and policies enacted meant to level the playing field, whites and blacks in many ways were growing farther apart. They had gone from separate pews to separate churches" (48). In fact, Emerson and Smith found that approximately 90 percent of congregations in America were at least 90 percent people of the same race. They argue that "in the face of social and religious pluralism, the organization of American religion powerfully drives religious groups toward internal similarity . . . to the extent that people can choose, they choose to be with people like themselves" (136). Due to this, Emerson and Woo (2006) find that Sunday mornings continue to be one of the most racially segregated times in the United States; however, they also note there has been an increase in multiracial congregations, which signals this could be changing.

According to more recent data from the Pew Research Center (2014), 75 percent of black people in the U.S. feel that religion is very important compared to only 49 percent of white people. Similarly, while about half (47 percent) of black people in the U.S. say they attend religious services at least once a week, only 34 percent of white people say they attend religious services at this rate (Pew Research Center 2014). Thus, black people in the United States today find religion more important and are more likely to be actively involved in a religious community than are white people.

Four of the six black trans men continued to identify as Christian, one as spiritual but not religious, and only one indicated that religion and spirituality were not important in their life. For instance, one black man, Lamar, avowed, "Religion is first. I feel like there's nothing that I can accomplish without my faith in God." On the contrary, only eight of 38 white trans men continued to identify as Christian, while half of the white trans men explained that religion and spirituality were not important aspects of their lives. Finally, of the seven respondents who identified as Hispanic, Indigenous, or multiracial, only one continued to identify as Christian, three identified as spiritual or as some other religion, and three explained that religion and spirituality were not important to them. While more research is needed to verify this trend, it appears that black trans men are more likely to find religion important to their lives and to be a part of a religious community, like the larger demographic surveys predict.

CONCLUDING THOUGHTS

This chapter provides an exploratory look into trans men's religious and spiritual beliefs and identities. Focusing on the Bible Belt, where religion, especially Protestant Christianity, continues to reign allows us to see the extent to which trans men are fleeing religious institutions, yet many maintain some sort of spirituality. A deeper analysis of trans men's spiritual beliefs would also add to the minimal research on trans religion and spirituality. Another potential area for future research is examining the beliefs and practices of trans men who remain within religious institutions. Abelson's (2014; 2016) research indicates that displaying white, heterosexual, manhood rewards some trans men in the South with a high degree of privilege. This raises the question of how trans men in the Bible Belt use this potential privilege within religious institutions.

Sumerau (2012) shows that cis gay men gain power and privilege within LGBTQ churches in the Southeast by partaking in compensatory manhood acts. Further inquiry is needed to determine if trans men also use hegemonic ideals of masculinity and compensatory manhood acts to gain power and control within religious institutions. For illustration, when Frank told his pastor he was trans, the pastor responded, "Alright, Bro. You are welcome to some of our men's studies. . . . If you ever feel uncomfortable around any of us, you know, the guys, just let me know." As a middle-aged white man, Frank was immediately welcomed into the fold and the pastor even told him he had his back. Being immediately welcomed into the men's groups and spaces will most likely confer privileges on Frank within the congregation, but further research is required to examine how trans men in this position use or handle this power and privilege.

Finally, research is necessary to understand the influence leaving religion has on trans men in the South. Identifying as Christian continues to bring power and privilege in the United States, and especially in the South. Unfortunately, research only rarely examines religion as an axis of inequality, like race, class, gender, and sexuality (Sumerau and Cragun 2018). This must be remedied, as religion remains a strong predictor of power in this country. Sumerau and Cragun (2018, xxii) note that religion, like these other vectors of inequality, is also "(1) something people do and create through their en-deavors, (2) something that may challenge or reproduce inequalities between people based on membership or claims of identity, and (3) something that one gains privilege from in contemporary American society." These characteristics of religion mean that "nonreligious people face considerable marginalization as a result of religious assumptions embedded throughout contemporary American families, political institutions, academic networks, friendship groups, legal systems, occupational markets, and healthcare systems" (xxiii). Therefore, they conclude, "religion—as a form of normativity capable of creating and sustaining inequalities itself—is central to understanding contemporary sexual and gender politics" (xxiii).

By leaving religion, trans men are losing ties to their communities and an identity that brings political and social rewards. The South remains a place where identity is judged largely by what church one attends. Almost all (98 percent) of the members of the 115th United States Congress (2017–2018) identified with a religion, and over 90 percent as Christian (Manning 2018). These numbers are even more pronounced in states within the Bible Belt. For example, 15 of Georgia's 16 members of Congress identified as Protestants in 2018. Likewise, all of the Congress members from South Carolina identified as Christian in 2018—eight Protestants and one Catholic. Clearly, religion remains an identity of privilege and power. If trans men are leaving religion at a higher rate than the general population this could put them at an even higher disadvantage politically and socially. In order to understand society, we have to understand religion and the power it has to shape all aspects of life in this country (Barrett-Fox 2016; Fetner 2008).

Chapter Six

Discord Within the Queer Community

"Gay men hate trans people."

—Mason—34-year-old Indigenous queer two-spirit person

Although some people assume the queer community is welcoming to everyone who does not identify as cis and heterosexual, this is not always the case. The queer community has not always been fully accepting of people who identify as bisexual (Curry 2014; Roberts, Horne, and Hoyt 2015); people who identify as trans or non-binary (Nash 2011; Rubin 2003; Sumerau et al. 2018); or people of color who identify as queer (Abelson 2016; Brooks 2016). For instance, Nash (2011) finds that trans men often feel they no longer belong in, or are pushed out of, the lesbian community after transition. Some men feel it is too "awkward to be read as butch (as opposed to 'male') within lesbian spaces" (200). Others are no longer comfortable or welcome in these predominantly women's spaces. In fact, some of Nash's respondents specifically discussed how hormones and surgeries were directly related to them being shunned within the lesbian bar scene. Before hormones and surgeries, some trans men could get by as "butch," but after physical transition began they were no longer welcomed into lesbian spaces by many women.

Similarly, Rowniak and Chesla (2013) find that for trans men who identified as lesbian before coming out as trans, being ostracized from the lesbian community was especially problematic. Of the trans men in Rowniak and Chesla's study, "many commented on the transphobia within the lesbian community and the feeling among some that transmen had betrayed the community" (452). After transition, many trans men find that they are no longer welcomed in the spaces where they once found community. This can be very problematic since many trans men's identities were initially shaped within lesbian spaces. Also, it is not clear which social spaces trans people fit into in the queer community. While trans men are sometimes accepted into gay men's spaces, there are limits to this acceptance as well. For example, Rowniak and Chesla (2013) explain that for trans men who identify as gay after transition, "the world of gay men was completely new and the rules and modus operandi apropos of sex and cruising were quite foreign. This had real implications for vulnerability regarding the ability to negotiate safe sex or even knowing how to assess and discuss risk" (454).

Another area where trans men have faced stigma and discrimination within the queer community is in drag kinging. In a previous study (Rogers 2018a), I find while the majority of trans drag kings find drag helpful for transition-ing, some kings faced problems when coming out as trans if they continued to perform drag. Almost a quarter of the drag kings in my study reported facing prejudice and discrimination within the drag community, or from the queer community at large (Rogers 2018a). The main issue was that trans men were still read as "being in drag," even outside of drag shows. The implica-tion being that true drag kings continued to be female-bodied, and to identify as women, outside of drag (Rogers 2018a). Additionally, some kings were shamed for continuing to perform masculinities after transition, claiming they were cheating because they now identified as men outside of drag.

In a study of trans students in college, Nicolazzo (2017) determined that the majority of lesbian, gay, bisexual, and queer spaces on college campuses also excluded trans people by becoming cisnormative. Relatedly, Sumerau et al. (2018, 11) find that while most heterosexual and asexual trans people had both positive and negative reactions from friends and family members when coming out, when they came out within the queer community they "noted experiences with LGBQ others that were mostly or entirely negative." There-fore, in a community where many trans people become themselves, they then face stigma for being themselves. Many of the respondents in this study found this reality particularly distressing and hoped to foster a queer community that is more accepting of all gender and sexual minorities.

FINDINGS: TRANS EXCLUSION

Nolan believed trans people were often excluded from the queer community because gender and sexuality are not the same thing: "I do believe [trans people] are quite frequently excluded because a majority of things that label themselves as LGBT resources definitely have more resources geared toward sexuality than they do geared towards gender. I think a lot that comes with people trying to lump those two things into the same category, and while they're related, they are not the same thing." Dayton, who identified his sexuality as pansexual, seconded this: "I'm always curious about why transgender is lumped in with LGBT anyways, since gender and sexuality are different things." And, Andre described it this way:

> Being gay or lesbian or bisexual has to do with who you sleep with, you know . . . who you're attracted to, and being trans is who you are, who you wake up as, and who you sleep as. . . . So, I think that a lot of people, even in the LGB community, that are not aware of what it means to be trans think that trans is kind of selling out and trying to be quote-unquote "normal or binary," or whatever you want to call it.

These responses demonstrate how the emphasis on education and media attention to sexuality have been largely successful, while many people, even in the queer community, remain uninformed and unconcerned with issues of gender identity.

Samuel felt that the exclusion of trans people from the queer community was more intentional and malicious than some of the other respondents. He thought trans people were excluded because they were "harder for straight people to understand and so it's easier to throw us under the bus than to include us sometimes." Samuel went on to explain that he felt that cis gay and lesbian people were assimilationist: "They want to act like they're closer to straight people than they are to us [trans people]." What Samuel was describing is homonormativity—a process "wherein lesbian and gay people who are willing and able to conform to heteronormative race, class, gender, family, religion, and marital statuses" are then able to "have their status in society elevated" (Duggan 2002; Sumerau and Cragun 2018, xxi). When monosexual gay and lesbian people attempt to appear more like cis straight people, they often ostracize trans people and other bi+ sexual minorities in the process. By throwing trans and bi+ people under the bus, cis gay men and cis lesbian women often gain the benefits of acceptance within cis heterosexual communities.

Carter agreed that lesbian, gay, and bisexual groups actively excluded trans people. He argued, being "gay or lesbian or bisexual, I don't think that it gives you any advantage on understanding [being trans] any more than a straight person. . . . I think that it's just when you are in a group that's oppressed by people, you tend to lash out at people within your own community because you can't really do that to people outside of your community cause you're already the underdog with them." Therefore, by siding with cis people, certain segments of the queer community gain some of the cis-heteronormative privileges; bargaining with the cis-heteronormative patriarchy allows cis queer people to gain some of the dividends of that privilege.

When it came to dating within the queer community, trans men also faced tremendous prejudice and discrimination. Darius said this was because gay men and lesbian women tied their sexual identities too closely to the genitaila of their preferred partner, rather than their gender identity and expression: "It's not just, 'I am attracted to people who look like this,' it's also, 'People who have this hardware.'" This made Darius especially concerned about being in queer spaces, because "gay men in particular are very particular about . . . who they like and what they're looking for. . . . You don't know when you walk into [queer] places and someone identifies as a gay man . . . if that person is a cool person who is attracted to men of all kinds, or if they are specifically looking for a dick." Donnie concurred; he explained that oftentimes he had issues dating cis lesbian women and cis gay men because they often felt that their sexual identities were threatened by dating a trans man. For Donnie, it may not have been that these cis gay men and cis lesbian woman were transphobic necessarily; rather, they could not understand their own identities in relation to someone who did not conform to the sex and gender binary. This is similar to what Pfeffer (2017) finds for some lesbian women in relationships with trans men.

Levi believed trans men were often excluded from the queer community because "most of us identify as straight, so we are seen as if we don't belong anymore. If you aren't gay or lesbian, then you are outside of the community." Maddox found a similar situation with the Gay Straight Alliance (GSA) on his college campus in Georgia. He and another trans man tried to join the GSA and felt they were

> ostracized for not being queer enough . . . I was dating this girl at the time and they were like, "Oh, well Maddox's like straight, he's dating a girl, like he doesn't count.". . . There was this push . . . to remove the S in GSA, they wanted no allies, no straight people allowed, and that included trans straight people, or trans people that were dating the opposite sex, or wanted a quote-unquote "straight relationship."

This theme of heterosexual trans people being excluded from the queer community came up time and time again. For some reason, the queer community in the South, even on college campuses among younger and presumably more liberal queer people, was interpreted to mean only sexual minorities. Similar to religion, the gains of cis gay men and cis lesbian women on college and university campuses did not necessarily translate to gains for trans people. Appearing cis and/or heterosexual was enough to have trans people ostracized from queer organizations across the region.

Gordon explained, "It's very sad when the community just discriminates against their own people," and Jace agreed that discrimination "hurts more" when it comes from within the queer community. Jace found it difficult to wrap his mind around how "people in the LGBT community who understand what prejudice is like . . . [could] still throw their opinions upon trans people, like they don't belong." Bruno explained that it was often trans people themselves who participated most in this prejudice and discrimination:

> Trans people are some of the most transphobic people I've ever met. It comes from internalizing a lot of the world around us and there's a lot of unlearning to be done. It hurts me, really hurts me to feel like there are men out there like, "I'm not trans," and that's fine, but I'm pretty sure you popped out of the womb with a vagina and there's nothing wrong with that.

In fact, eight of the men specifically mentioned prejudice and discrimination from other trans people as a major issue they had to deal with. Clearly, trans men, and all queer people, are part of the problematic systems of homophobia, heterosexism, transphobia, cisnormativity, etc. Being part of a minority in no way makes you an expert on the entire population, nor does it mean that you cannot be a part of the larger structural systems that are harming your own community.

Cis Gay Men & Spaces

Of the 51 trans men interviewed, 29 discussed facing prejudice and discrimination from cis gay men. These respondents felt strongly that the majority of prejudice and discrimination against trans men within the queer community comes from cis gay men. The respondents explained that gay men: 1) excluded trans men from the community, 2) did not see trans men as "real" men, 3) fetishized trans men, and 4) openly sexually harassed and assaulted trans men. These issues led a number of respondents to state unequivocally that "gay men are the worst." I will discuss the first three themes concerning cis gay men here; I will talk more about sexual harassment and assault in the next chapter.

Exclusion from the Queer Community

When I asked Timothy if he had faced prejudice or discrimination in the queer community, he said, "Oh god, yes. That's probably the worst. And I hate to say it because we are one big community, and we all should accept and love one another, but there's just something about gay men, gay cisgender men." Damien, who identified as pansexual, explained the worst is "freaking being misgendered by cis gay men, or ignored and disregarded." Overall, the men in this study felt that cis gay men ignored them or, worse, openly discriminated against them.

Mason believed that trans people should not be a part of the LGBTQ community, because they are treated so unfairly within the community and their needs are completely overlooked. He explained, "Gay men hate trans people. . . . Gay people aren't our allies . . . I'm part of the movement that wants to split the T from the LGB, because once they get what they need, they leave us out and waiting. I'm not saying all gay people, but a majority of those in power don't fight for trans folks." Mason's argument is related to the argument against the larger LGBTQ Civil Rights Movement, which for a long time has ignored the rights of trans people, as well as other groups, such as working-class queers and queers of color in the U.S. While these groups are expected to be committed to the movement, issues that affect their lives are often ignored when goals of the movement are being laid out.

Trans Men as "Real" Men

The next issue that came up repeatedly in regard to cis gay men was the belief that trans men were not "real" men. When I asked about discrimination and prejudice in the queer community, Alec, who identified as straight, said, "I think gay men more than anything [discriminate]. . . . There are some gay men that will never see a trans person, or a trans man, as a man." Damien also felt that to cis gay men, "I am less than a man, because I don't have a fucking penis; since I don't have a penis, I don't count." Similarly, for Garrett, a pansexual trans guy, gay men were the "worst" when it came to dating, because they are too concerned with genitalia: "I've never found a man that I wanted to date, because they're just completely an asshole about it. All they see is my body parts. They don't care about my personality and they just don't give a shit."

Gay men were often very blunt with trans men about these prejudices they held. Jace said, "I have found that gay men are the highest people to complain about transgender people. . . . I have had numerous gay men, especially if I'm at Pride, who will just be outright saying, 'Just stop what you're doing and try to be your gender you were assigned at birth, whatever your genitals you have is what you are.'" Timothy also had an issue when he was "crushing real hard" on a gay man; they were hanging out and the cis gay man said, "Well, honestly? I just don't really see you as a real dude."

Fetishizing Trans Men

Another related issue, according to Levi and some of the other men, was that often cis gay men were "into it"—having relationships or sex with trans men. Levi and others found this to be very degrading. Levi explained that many gay men "look at trans men as something to experience or learn about, but not as people. He went on, "A lot of trans women now want to date trans men . . . because they say we are nicer or better partners than gay men. Some gay men want to date us too. . . . It's like we are not people, but something to explore." Maddox also felt gay men fetishized him: "They're the quickest to fetishize . . . the quickest to make comments about how we're the whole package, especially bisexual men will say that kind of thing. . . . White gay men are just the worst." Jace believed gay men often discriminate against trans men because they feel threatened by them: "Maybe [gay men] feel like, well there is a theory that they're afraid we are taking all of the men from them . . . because we are quote-unquote 'The best of both worlds' . . . which is transphobic and not even accurate." Garrett even explained that one gay man said to him, "I've always wanted to try a trans." Garrett felt that, to cis gay men, trans men are "either a bucket list [item], or . . . not man enough."

Cis Lesbian Women & Spaces

Almost half (23 of 51) of the respondents had also faced prejudice or discrimination from cis lesbian women. This was particularly detrimental because the majority of trans men in this study (29 of 51) identified as lesbians at some point prior to transition, and an additional nine respondents identified as bisexual prior to transition. The majority of respondents were once part of the lesbian community and many frequented lesbian spaces prior to transitioning. However, a quarter of the respondents (13 of 51) no longer felt comfortable in lesbian spaces, and many avoided these spaces at all costs. There were three primary themes that came out of the data regarding trans men and cis lesbian women and spaces: 1) animosity towards trans men, 2) dating lesbians, and 3) infringing on women's spaces.

"You're a Traitor": Animosity Towards Trans Men

Lots of the trans men I talked with felt intense hostility from cis lesbian women after coming out as trans. According to Nolan, "The most common phrase I've heard is what they call a feminazi, like feminists who are so die-hard feminist that they look at trans men as like a betrayal of feminism, and it's not. It has nothing to do with that." Nolan was not the only man to feel this tension and be seen as a betrayal to women. Jeffrey said that most of his negative experiences in the queer community were with cis lesbian women: "Lesbians are not happy that people transition or the female-to-male transition. I've been told things like, 'You're a traitor,' or 'You're giving up on women,' or 'You're trying to enjoy the benefits of being a man.'" Similarly, Bruno said, "A lot of butch lesbians, they kinda call me 'a gender traitor,' and they say I'm 'a homophobic lesbian.'" Damien said some "women view being a man as a betrayal, yet the men don't view me as a man. They got shit twisted in their heads." In addition to being called a gender traitor, some trans men experienced their identities being invalidated by cis lesbian women who did not believe that trans is an actual identity. Carter explained that some lesbian women "think that you're just kind of making something up or that you're like a traitor in some way." Trans men are thus viewed with suspicion from both cis men and cis women. The theme of not being "real" continues to emerge out of the queer community; trans men are not "real" men, trans is not a "real" identity, and yet, they are not "real" women because they are traitors to the gender. These beliefs clearly leave trans men feeling excluded and discriminated against within the queer community.

For many of the men I spoke with, as soon as they began to identify as trans, they were pushed out of the lesbian community. Trip put it this way: "It's like now I'm no longer a lesbian . . . like as soon as I could pass for a straight man, I was ostracized from [the lesbian] community. . . . Because I pass as a straight guy, look like a straight guy, act like a straight guy through their eyes, they don't want to have anything to do with me." So, where do trans men fit? What community do they belong to?

Trans men's experiences with cis lesbian women were often related to lesbian and feminist prejudices against trans people, which in popular culture, many refer to as trans exclusionary radical feminists (TERFs). Often, these feminists view trans women as threatening to women's spaces, and view trans men as traitors who are giving up on women to gain privilege. Research (Newton 2018; Stein 2018), and my own anecdotal experience (Rogers 2018b), demonstrate that TERFs are often lesbians. These cis lesbian women feel trans men are depleting the queer community of masculine/butch lesbians, and potential dating partners. For some reason, these often older lesbian women feel a sense of entitlement to having butch lesbians available for their dating pleasures.

Dating Lesbians

These prejudices within the lesbian community obviously led many trans men to be cautious when it came to dating cis lesbian women. For example, Samuel felt strongly about lesbians, saying, "I've had bad experiences with lesbians. . . . If you identify as a lesbian, don't fucking hit on me. Like, I have a fucking beard . . . and don't throw a hissy fit when I tell you I'm a fucking man and I'm not interested in dating lesbians. It's really easy, I think. But, yeah, I just hate that shit." Andre also felt that he had faced the most prejudice when attempting to date cis lesbian women. He said one especially problematic experience he had was "when a woman who identifies as a lesbian and says that she's attracted to me, but she's not attracted to men, she's interested in only dating trans men. . . . It brings out my dysphoria even more because I feel like she's attracted to things that I don't like about myself." Again, cis lesbian women were either viewing trans men as a betrayal to women or still viewing them as women. Garrett explained, "I know that lesbians are very transphobic, as far as towards trans women . . . [but] they'll still go after trans men because they still view them as women still, cause it's, you know, hashtag vagina." Much like with cis gay men, Garrett felt fetishized as the "best of both worlds."

Infringing on Women's Spaces

In terms of lesbian spaces, Mason explained that after beginning his transition in Arkansas, "I lost all of my lesbian friends"; therefore, he began to "silo" himself to only "TPOC [trans people of color] spaces." Similarly, Ronald lost some friends when he came out as trans: "All of those friends were lesbians. So, I started to remove myself from the lesbian groups. . . . I realized I didn't fit anymore; I felt like I was infiltrating their space."

For Bruno, lesbian spaces were never a place he felt comfortable. He said, "I never hung out in lesbian bars . . . I'm not a woman and I don't need to infringe on women's spaces. Like that's really none of my business." Zac agreed with Bruno: "I would feel a little uncomfortable being in a lesbian place because I would feel like I was intruding. . . . I would be afraid that I was making them uncomfortable by being in a traditionally women dominated space." Lots of the respondents spoke of infringing on women's spaces in lesbian bars; however, some trans men felt torn over this because many identified as lesbians before they transitioned. This meant the men had to choose whether or not to give up a space where they once felt accepted and safe.

On the other hand, Sage, who identified as queer, still felt more comfortable in lesbian bars than gay bars. He explained that most of his friends were women and trans people: "I don't really have a lot of cis men friends." Nevertheless, Sage did say that when he's in a lesbian bar, "I still feel a bit anxious and like self-doubting, like, do they think I'm a lesbian or a man?" Hayden also told me, "All my best friends are lesbians, so, yeah I've ventured to a lot of lesbian hangouts a lot of times."

Some other respondents avoided lesbian spaces, but not out of fear of intruding. For instance, Samuel declared, "I would absolutely not feel comfortable in a lesbian space. I would rather fucking, like slit my fucking wrist than hang out in a lesbian space. . . . I would not set foot in a fucking lesbian space at this point in my life." A couple of respondents, like Samuel, felt that going into a cis lesbian space would mean they would be read as women, or be hit on by lesbian women. For these men, neither of these options would be good for their mental health and self-perception. Being hit on by lesbian women meant to them that they were somehow not being read fully as men, since lesbians were assumed to only be interested in women.

Other Prejudices in the Queer Community

As I have discussed throughout this book, intersectionality plays an important role in all aspects of our lives. Not only were the interviewees trans men, they also each had a race, a sexuality, a socioeconomic class, and many other interesting characteristics. Therefore, many of the respondents felt excluded from the queer community not because, or only because, they were trans men, but due to other aspects of their identities.

Class

Mason explained that although white cis gay men were the main problem in the queer community for him, white cis lesbian women and white trans women also ignored the needs of others in the community. He said, "It's not just about the fact that we identify as far as our gender is concerned, it's also socioeconomic and class, so there's a lot of classism and marginalization happening. More affluent folks I don't think are allies as one would think they should be." Maddox had also experienced classism in the queer community: "Trans folks that can easily afford transition services will discriminate against those who can't easily afford transition services. Because in their minds it's easy. . . . So, they'll just be like, 'Oh, you're just making excuses, work harder.'" This is highly related to the issues of transnormativity discussed previously in Chapter 3.

Race

Most of the men of color explained they had faced racism in the queer community. For instance, Andre said:

> Especially in the South . . . I'm always boxed up depending on who knows me and how much they know about me. Some people only see me as a black man, some people only see me as an immigrant, some people only see me as an undocumented immigrant, some people see me as trans, some trans people see me as heteronormative.

Damien, who identified as multiracial, said that most of the problems he had in the queer community had been with "old white racist gays," a group he referred to as the "KKGays." He said this group of white cis gay men "don't wanna see they're privileged . . . when someone says something's fucked up, they're like, 'Oh, they didn't mean it like that.' I'm like, 'Yes, you did.'"

Sexuality

Jamar, who identified as pansexual, explained that he and his wife faced prejudice in the queer community based on their sexuality. They identified as poly and were told by a trans woman, "That doesn't count, that would make you just a slut, because you're with multiple people." Jace identified as bisexual, and said, "It's kind of ironic . . . I am a bisexual trans man, because there's the part of the LGBT community that doesn't accept trans men and then there's the part that doesn't even acknowledge bisexual people, so, it's kind of like, I'm just kind of there." Both Jamar and Jace faced prejudice due to mononormativity within the queer community. According to Sumerau and Cragun (2018, 33), "Mononormativity is an ideology that asserts that (1) all people are only one sexuality throughout their lives (monosexism), and (2) all people are only sexually active with one partner at a time (compulsory monogamy)." They argue that "mononormative assumptions pervade contemporary social, political, sexual, religious, and even scientific norms in contemporary America" (34). In fact, these assumptions are so pervasive, they also invade sexual and gender minority communities. These mononormative assumptions lead to the belief that poly and bi+ sexualities are not real and people who identify as poly and/or bi+ are untrustworthy, selfish, and immoral. Additionally, mononormativity prevades in cis gay and lesbian through the battle for same-sex marriage, which often uses ideas of gay and lesbian couples being just like "good and moral" straight couples, meaning monogamous—making a commitment to only one partner at a time.

Jamie faced prejudice in the queer community based on his sexuality as well. He said most of the prejudice he faced in the queer community was for identifying as gay: "Oddly enough, a trans man being gay was very weird for the queer community here." He explained that people started asking his boyfriend if he (Jamie) was straight now that he was dating a man. Jamie chalked this up mostly to "a lot of ignorance . . . more than anything else." Darius, who identified as asexual, said he had definitely faced prejudice in the queer community for "identifying as ace, just cause so many people don't understand that. I feel like most people have some kind of like sexual urge or sexual desire." He clarified that much of the gay bar scene is about sex and finding sexual partners, so he found it safer to avoid it altogether. Garrett, who identified as pansexual, also believed as a trans guy it's best to avoid the bar scene because of the "whole predatory nature" of the bar and everyone is just there "trying to hook up." Finally, Parker, who identified as asexual, said, "I don't really tell people often that I'm asexual because I worry about that. . . . From my perspective, everyone like really loves sex and I think the idea of someone not being super into it is like mind-boggling, they just like sort of freak out a little bit."

CONCLUDING THOUGHTS

Despite the prejudice and discrimination found in the queer community, most of the trans men I spoke with also found support in some places within this community. For Alec, there were many prejudices between cis gay men, cis lesbian women, and trans people, but in the end he believed, "When we need to come together, we do, when we need to have each other's back, we do, and that's all that matters. I think we could do without the drama and bullshit, but you know, everybody's gotta have that one person. I like to call her Karen." Emmett, a lifelong Southerner who resided in rural Arkansas, said that because the queer community was so small where he lives, "everybody kinda supports everybody." This again demonstrates the importance that future research continue to take seriously the lives of rural queer people. The bigger the queer community in an area, the more divisions emerge. In communities where there were not enough people to form various cliques within the queer community, queer people were more likely to get along and support one another. As Emmett said, "We pretty much only got each other."

Chapter Seven

Sexual Harassment and Assault

"I could fix you with just one good dick session."

—Comment made to an interviewee

The majority of research to date concerning sexual harassment and assault focuses on the experiences of women, predominately cis women. This chapter broadens our understanding of sexual harassment and assault by examining trans men's experiences. Little research, outside of counseling literature, considers trans people's experiences with sexual harassment and assault (Jauk 2013; Stotzer 2009). The research that does exist does little to differentiate between the experiences of trans women and trans men. The scarce research that does examine sexual violence against trans people shows high rates of sexual harassment and assault and demonstrates the tremendous physical health and mental health effects of sexual violence against this already vulnerable population.

In a national survey of trans individuals living in the U.S., Grant et al. (2011) find trans people experience higher incidences of sexual assault than their cis peers. For instance, in K–12 education, 12 percent of trans and nonbinary students reported sexual assault, including 3 percent reporting sexual assault by teachers and school staff. In the workplace, about 6 percent of trans people report experiencing sexual assault. These statistics are especially pertinent considering the fact that 41 percent of trans people have attempted suicide, compared to 1.6 percent of the general population (Clements-Nolle et al. 2006; Grant et al. 2011; Miller and Grollman 2015). The percentage of trans individuals who attempt suicide increases dramatically, to 64 percent, after experiencing sexual assault.

This examination of trans men's experiences with sexual harassment and assault in the South adds to the conversation about sexual violence against trans men and begins to assess the following questions: 1) Does sexual violence perpetrated against trans men differ before and after gender transition? 2) How does being recognized as a man relate to sexual harassment and assault? 3) Do cis men use sexual harassment and assault as a means of holding trans men accountable for doing masculinity in stereotypical ways?

By exploring how trans men's experiences differ based on whether they are recognized as women or men, this data demonstrates the utmost importance of gender and power in regards to sexual violence. While research shows trans women are more likely to experience sexual assault than trans men (Grant el al. 2011), and more research is needed to understand trans women's experiences with sexual violence, trans men's experiences with sexual harassment and assault demonstrate how being read as a man diminishes incidences of sexual violence. Still, almost all of the trans men interviewed for this study (45 of 51) experienced sexual harassment or assault at some point in their lives. Therefore, the lack of research and activism regarding sexual violence against trans men in an inexcusable oversight.

According to a study conducted by a non-profit organization, Stop Street Harassment, 81 percent of cis women and 43 percent of cis men have experienced some form of sexual harassment, ranging from verbal comments, such as catcalling, to physically aggressive forms of harassment, such as following, groping, or flashing (Chatterjee 2018; Stop Street Harassment 2014). Compared to cis heterosexual men, gay, bisexual, and trans men report higher rates of sexual harassment. For illustration, 57 percent of gay, bisexual, and trans men report verbal harassment, compared to 37 percent of cis heterosexual men. Similarly, 45 percent of gay, bisexual, and trans men report physically aggressive harassment, compared to 28 percent of cis heterosexual men (Stop Street Harassment 2014).

The National Sexual Violence Resource Center (NSVRC 2019) explains that approximately one out of every three women and one out of every six men have experienced sexual violence at some point in their lives. In regard to sexual assault in the form of rape, NSVRC reports one out of every five women and one out of 71 men have experienced a completed rape. A large proportion of sexual violence occurs before the age of 18 for both girls and boys. One out of four girls and one out of six boys experience sexual abuse before the age of 18 (NSVRC 2019). The statistics for sexual violence among trans people are more difficult to obtain due to lack of data collection and unfair treatment of trans and non-binary people by the justice system. However, the Rape, Abuse, and Incest National Network (RAINN 2019) reports that 21 percent of trans, genderqueer, and gender non-conforming college students have been sexually assaulted, compared to 18 percent of cis women and 4 percent of cis men.

Overall, the men I spoke with described "common" incidences of sexual harassment and assault before being recognized as men, such as catcalling, obscene sexual comments, and unwanted touching (Mitchell et al. 2014). Once trans men began to identify as men, and more importantly began to be *recognized* as men, the occurrences of sexual harassment and assault changed, and mostly decreased. For trans men who are recognized as men, sexual violence began to revolve more around rejection of binary gender expectations—specifically, holding them accountable to stereotypical displays of masculinity—and minority sexual identities (Miller and Grollman 2015). Sexual harassment and assault was carried out after transition in order to try to force trans men back into the sex category they were assigned at birth and into a subordinate gender—women. As I have demonstrated throughout this book, this is also important because we know that trans men's fear of crime has a major influence on how they perform masculinities (Abelson 2014). Trans men perform more hegemonic and toxic masculinities when they perceive a situation as dangerous. Therefore, understanding trans men's perceptions of fear and safety is important for creating spaces where trans men can enact more transformative masculinities.

FINDINGS: SEXUAL HARASSMENT, SEXUAL ASSAULT, AND RAPE BY THE NUMBERS

Thirty-four of the 51 trans men I interviewed reported sexual harassment prior to transitioning—when they were being recognized as girls or women. Following transition—when they were recognized as men—19 respondents indicated they had experienced sexual harassment. This decreased prevalence of sexual harassment is likely due to the fact that many of the men began to pass as cis men and identify as heterosexual following transition. Of the 36 trans men who experienced sexual harassment at some point in their lives, 23 indicated they mostly, or only, experienced sexual harassment prior to transition. In total, only 15 respondents had never experienced sexual harassment.

Overall, the trans men in this study also reported much higher rates of sexual assault and rape than the national averages predict. Over half of the respondents (27 of 51) experienced some form of sexual assault prior to transition and being recognized as men. Thirteen men discussed incidences of childhood sexual abuse. Fifteen men reported sexual assault that they classified as rape. Following transition—once the respondents were recognized as men—the incidences of sexual violence dropped drastically. Since transitioning, seven respondents had experienced sexual assault or rape. Obviously, the amount of time before and after transition was not equal; some respondents had identified as trans for decades, while a couple respondents still were not out as trans to most people. Nonetheless, the men felt that experiencing less sexual violence after transition was to be expected and would continue. In fact, some of the men no longer feared sexual violence after being recognized as men. Only 19 men had never experienced sexual assault or rape, before or after transition. These men, who had not experienced sexual violence, understood how commonplace sexual assault and rape are in our society and considered themselves lucky.

Childhood Sexual Violence

As mentioned, while most of the men had experienced sexual violence during their lives, the vast majority of this violence took place while they identified as, or were recognized as, girls or women. Many respondents discussed sexual violence experienced as children, often at the hands of older cis men who were relatives or friends of the family. Frank discussed an incidence of sexual harassment that occurred when he was around 14: "It was my mom's great friend, who I guess he just felt that if you were a female in the household, well I guess that he had the right to openly comment on your physical attributes . . . or your genitalia." Rowen explained that he was sexually assaulted and raped between the ages of four and eight by three different men—his best friend's older brother, his father's friend, and a man that lived in his father's apartment building. Another respondent, Ronald, told me he had "been raped at least three times." He explained that he lost his virginity to rape at 15 and was constantly sexually harassed when he was being recognized as a young woman. Ronald said, "I don't trust cisgender men; cisgender men are ruled by their dick." Finally, Jorge was sexually assaulted by his best friend's dad who told him that he was gonna make him "be the woman that [he] was born as." At the time, Jorge was ten and presenting as a tomboy.

Catcalling and Inappropriate Behavior

Most respondents experienced sexual harassment or assault that they described as "common" to the experience of living as a girl or woman in our society. In fact, many downplayed this type of harassment as to be expected, or nothing out of the ordinary. For instance, Jayden said, "You obviously get, people get catcalled and things like that, but things of that nature, I mean, yeah it's harassment, but it's not something that like I'm putting in my book like, 'I was harassed today.'" Or, Eli, a 19-year-old white gay transgender person, put it this way when asked about sexual harassment: "Nothing serious, just lots of comments from men, like typical street harassment, I guess catcalling and that sort of thing." Bruno described:

I was sexually assaulted when I was younger and that sort of thing, but it was all very like typical of the female experience and that, you know, that's sad to say that there's that experience, but it was, it was all very, very typical. And just based on the fact that they looked at me and saw a girl and so they saw a target and that's what a lot of the behavior is like.

Finally, Dakota explained that prior to transition he did not face the same degree of sexual violence: "I mean like, you know, the typical shit in high school, like high school boys, I don't even, that sounds terrible, but like nothing that stands out the way [other experiences after transition] did."

Jamar received a lot of unwanted attention at work because he was "forced to dress female" for his job. He said that the uniform

caused me to be a target, a type of target I didn't want to be. . . . I didn't desire to have that kind of male interaction. Even though I would bind my chest and try to feel as masculine as I could, they still only saw me as female. And so, I would get hit on. I had actual advancements by supervisors that if I didn't do this or that, that I wouldn't have a job.

Other respondents also discussed sexual harassment in the workplace and how their jobs and careers were influenced by this harassment. Being forced to wear women's clothing, go by their dead names, or being outed at work put many trans men in danger of further harassment and discrimination.

You're Not a Lesbian, You Just Haven't Met the Right Man

The majority (43 of 51) of respondents came out as gay, lesbian, or bi+ prior to their gender transitions. A lot of the sexual violence they experienced during this time was meant to prove to them that they were not gay, lesbian, or bi+. They were harassed and assaulted with the explicit goal of proving to them they were confused about their sexual identity. Alec faced sexual harassment when he identified as a lesbian: "As far as being trans and being sexually harassed, no. I dealt with it more as a lesbian . . . men wanna be like, 'All you need is a good dickin',' or some shit like that." Jace had a similar experience when he was first starting his transition from a lesbian identity to a trans identity: "A guy I used to work with at my old job would always make these lewd side comments about how, 'You just need a really good dick, you don't need all this [trans stuff].' He was like, 'I could fix you with just one good dick session.'" While many of the trans men were verbally harassed when they came out as lesbians, Emmett experienced sexual assault to prove to him he was not a lesbian. Emmett told me that he came out as a lesbian when he was 13 years old and soon after, "a close family friend," who was 25, raped him "to prove that [he] was not a lesbian."

Sexual Violence Against Trans Men

Although the majority of sexual violence occurred prior to transition, some of the respondents experienced sexual violence after being recognized as men. This violence was often perpetrated with the stated objective of proving they were not "real" men. Some of the respondents' experiences with sexual violence after transition were especially unique in light of the current literature, and is another reason why further research is required to fully understand the dynamics of sexual violence against trans men. Particularly, while the vast majority of the sexual violence prior to transition was carried out by perpetrators who were cis heterosexual men, after transition much of the violence against the men was carried out by cis gay men and trans women.

Nolan was sexually harassed by cis heterosexual men after his transition, but believed these men were "probably threatened" by him; they would "comment to say how they were probably more adequately equipped to please a lady." However, Nolan said the majority of sexual violence he dealt with after transitioning came from cis gay men:

> The worst that usually happens to me is that people . . . [mostly] gay men . . . tend to get real gropey and touchy-feely without making sure it's okay. I don't know what it is about being a trans man that makes people think it's okay. It's kind of like being pregnant and people thinking it's okay to touch the mama's belly, it's kind of like that with trans men and their packers and their chests. A lot of times people think that if a trans guy has had chest surgery then it must be okay for you to just reach up and touch their chest or feel their chest and it's really not. Just like anything else, it should require consent.

Levi concurred that people felt emboldened to touch his body inappropriately after transitioning:

> After transition a lot of the [sexual harassment] has been from trans women and gay men. I've been asked inappropriate questions; questions that are no one's business, like, "Do you have a penis?" I've also been touched inappropriately. They grab your crotch or touch my chest like I don't feel anything there. . . . [Also] I've had women inappropriately proposition me at work at multiple jobs.

Andre shared a similar experience and explained that most of the sexual violence he faced since transitioning came from trans women and cis lesbian women. He described an incident when he was asked by a woman whether he had physically transitioned, "but I didn't even have the chance to answer and she was already grabbing me, and it was in public, that was like very uncomfortable." Carter discussed a "big group of guys . . . just like talking about my genitals and my private parts." He went on to explain they were all cis gay men and they were "talking about how they would like to still have sex with me, because of this or that reason, or like they were describing the ways they would do it." Ronald said trans women harassed him all the time since transitioning, but went on to say that he doesn't see it the same as he did when he was being harassed by cis men: "You know, some trans women have penises, but they aren't as aggressive as cis men." Finally, Hayden described "getting clawed by a gay man." When I asked him to explain, he said that "the claw was basically they reached underneath, like, between my legs and like grab your junk and then they come back and they kind of get one finger towards your butt-hole. So, yeah, that happened to me." He said that sexual violence was "totally different once you transition. . . . Just the gay men, they're the ones you gotta watch out for nowadays."

Still, some trans men continued to face sexual violence from cis heterosexual men after transition, often with the explicit purpose of proving they were not "real" men. Dakota had two such experiences with sexual violence after transitioning. At the age of 22, Dakota was raped while he was passed out at a party. The perpetrator knew he was trans, and when he woke up the perpetrator said, "Well, a real guy would never let that happen." Later, Dakota faced sexual harassment at work from a male coworker who continuously asked him to have sex; the coworker said that he wanted to have sex with him because "it doesn't make me gay . . . you're not a full dude."

CONCLUDING THOUGHTS

Overall, the men indicated they felt much safer from sexual violence after transitioning and the numbers supported their lowered levels of fear. Most of the incidences of sexual harassment and assault experienced by the men occurred before they began to be recognized as men. Dayton explained that since transitioning sexual harassment was something "I don't worry about at all anymore." He said that he is no longer "being viewed as a sexual object, or feeling like I need to be one." Damien concurred; since transitioning, sexual harassment "happens to me a lot less. So, that is one benefit."

Even as the rate of sexual violence decreased after transition for some men, there remains a lack of resources for those who continue to face sexual harassment and assault as trans men. Due to issues of toxic masculinity and harassment by police and medical practitioners, when trans men are sexually harassed and assaulted they often do not feel comfortable reporting the violence and seeking care. Mason told me there is a huge gap in resources and understanding sexual assault and rape against trans men, which he believed was caused by a number of factors:

> I think partly, we internalize because, you know . . . it's hard for me to say that I was assaulted by a woman, and the perception of that and how we're seen . . . "You let a woman rape you?" . . . It makes it hard for [trans men] to talk about our sexual assaults, and I know trans men deal with a great bit of sexual assault and rape, that we just don't talk about because of toxic masculinity. I have several friends who have been assaulted. . . . Showing up to an ER (emergency room) for a rape, we don't get treated like the 19-year-old college sorority girl, who gets cared for and resources. We just get whatever STI test and pregnancy test and shoved out the door. So, in those medical institutions we're not cared for physically or mentally as we should be, and we have the stigma, the social stigma of it, that we just find it easier to not talk about it, and I think that, along with how we feel about our own bodies, [leads us to avoid care].

The vast majority of men I spoke with did not get justice for the sexual violence perpetrated against them. However, Jorge made clear in his interview that these men should not be viewed as victims, but as survivors of a broken culture and system. As researchers and activists, we must use these brave survivors' stories to address the issue of sexual violence against trans men, and everyone, an issue that has for too long been ignored and under-resourced. We must stand in solidarity with these men and demand change.

Conclusion

In this study, I answer the call for more research on the lives of queer people in the Southeast, and in rural areas of the country more generally. I demonstrate the importance of geographic location, the South, rural areas, and ordinary cities (Johnson et al. 2016; Stone 2018) when considering trans men's experiences. By further nuancing our understanding of trans men in the South—a location with elevated minority stressors, we can expand our understandings of gender and masculinities, along with a myriad of other issues trans men must deal with, including prejudice, discrimination, oppression, and sexual violence. Fitting into the gender binary through passing and engaging in compensatory manhood acts makes life more livable for many trans men in this region. Claims of sameness allow some trans men to carry out their lives in the South in a *relatively* privileged and safe way. This explains why many trans men opt to stay in the South, even when options to leave are available. Trans men's presentations of masculinities and ruralities make them feel more comfortable in the South and in rural areas, despite the downfalls of conservative religion, racism, and toxic masculinity in these areas.

At the same time, this research unequivocally demonstrates our society has not moved to an inclusive form of masculinity, and why geographic location and intersecting identities must be centered in research on marginalized populations. In the South, masculinities remain largely tied to heterosexuality, stereotypical manhood acts, privilege, and inequality. Even when "doing transgender," many trans men in this region fail to develop a "feminist consciousness" (C. Connell 2010), largely due to the constraints placed on the "proper" presentation of masculinity in the region. My respondents more closely align with some of Schilt's (2006) who did not develop a feminist consciousness from passing as men. As Schilt puts it, "Having a critical perspective on gender discrimination . . . is not inherent" to trans men's experiences (474). Negative characteristics of Southern masculinity related to aggression, treatment of women, and homophobia mean that many trans men must decide between being accepted as "one of the boys," or a feminist consciousness that allows them to develop a masculinity not solely based on the oppression of others. As Schilt and C. Connell (2007) explain, people around trans men play a large role in forcing them to "do gender," rather than "cause gender trouble"; anxieties around gender "result in a reinforcement of binary views on gender through the reproduction of gendered hierarchies that disadvantage women and rigid adherence to the 'right' way to do gender" (614). That is, in order to fit in, receive privileges, and not disrupt systems, many trans men choose, or are forced, to present gender in stereotypical ways. Of course, these expectations also vary based on other intersecting characteristics, such as race and class.

The Southeast is a microcosm of the U.S. more broadly. Studying rural queers in the South offers a glimpse into this region, but into rural queer lives more generally. We should be using rural areas as a model of social justice for the broader country. While rurality is often characterized as backwards, conservative, and slow, it is the "slowness" of rural areas that allows the time to think and practice empathy in ways that those living in more fast-paced, urban areas often miss. Also, somewhat counterintuitively, with fewer people and more face-to-face contact, rural areas often prove to be a place where difference is more accepted. Maybe queer lives are not accepted in a waving your flag kind of way, but queers are known and accepted in their families, churches, and communities across the rural U.S. (Johnson 2008) Granted, this may be a conditional acceptance (Rogers 2019b) or based on "claims of sameness" (Abelson 2016a), but the fact that queer people are integrated into most rural communities suggests something is working. As Kazyak (2012) argues, rural areas may in fact offer more ways of being, particularly for those who do masculinities, such as lesbians, and in this case trans men. Additionally, within the queer community, some trans men found more acceptance in small communities than those in larger, urban areas. When the queer community is smaller, everyone must depend on one another for support. When there are not enough queer people to create cliques and ostracize one another, we listen to one another, work together, and seek to improve the lives of the community, not just our own lives.

Trans men's stories allow us to better understand and interrogate gender, particularly masculinities, in our culture. These stories demonstrate that we are all human, and constrained by the social structures we have created, and continue to recreate daily. As individuals we have agency to challenge institutions and structures; however, in order to challenge constricting systems—masculinity, transnormativity, religion, homophobia, heteronormativity, sexual violence, etc.—we must acknowledge them, educate ourselves about them, and stand together for a more just and equitable future.

Moving Forward

As an activist and sociologist, I strongly believe that the divide between activism and scholarship has been perpetuated by those with power in order to keep marginalized groups from accessing that power. Sociologists must, at a minimum, provide suggestions for bettering the worlds we study; otherwise we are only taking advantage of our subjects to further our careers. As Jane Addams and Ida B. Wells-Barnett, early feminist sociologists, explained, social science without morality and a commitment to bettering our social world is a waste of time, especially for vulnerable populations who need resources and change in the present. By "writing out" these early feminists, activists, and sociologists from the canon of sociology in the late nineteenth and early twentieth centuries, we arrived at a place in the academy where "true science" was seen as separate from social work and activism. Like Travers (2018) and many before them, I call for a social action model of research. A model that, "unlike traditional, and inaccurate, portrayals of science and academic research being characterized by so-called objectivity and lack of invested interest, the social action model of research is explicitly designed to develop knowledge that can be used to fight oppression." We must bring back the influence of our action-oriented founders and push for a model of research that takes the fight against oppression seriously.

With this is mind, I offer my perspective on what is needed to create a more equitable and just world for trans men (and all vulnerable populations), especially those living in the Southeast. Based on this research, I argue that the following three suggestions can improve the social world of trans men in the South: 1) provide education about trans people and issues; 2) respect people's choices about their own lives—which includes ensuring that individuals have the material resources to make informed choices; and 3) teach and practice empathy.

Provide Education

Many respondents in this study explained that the problems they faced, particularly in the South, were related to a lack of education around trans issues in the region. They believed that a lack of education led others in their communities to hold negative perceptions of trans people, and led to a complete misunderstanding of who they were as people. This lack of education was especially important and pronounced when it came to healthcare professionals. Many of the men I spoke to had to search for hours on end to find healthcare providers, drive long distances to reach healthcare providers who would serve them, and then still educate their healthcare providers about what it means to be trans, including the type of healthcare they needed regarding transition, but also basic things, such as calling people by the name and pronouns they prefer.

Importantly, this education on trans issues must mirror feminist calls and provide information from multiple standpoints. Foremost, education on trans issues must include the voices of trans people. Even in these tumultuous political and social times, individuals, and especially educators with privilege, must use education "as the practice of freedom" (hooks 1994). Professors must incorporate trans people and trans issues into all of our courses. Teachers in K–12 education must be knowledgeable about issues of gender and sexuality, and teach students about equality and inclusion. Medical professionals must take initiative to educate themselves, and those around them, in order to provide fair and adequate treatment for trans people. hooks clearly delineates "the difference between education as the practice of freedom and education that merely strives to reinforce domination" (4). Educators, including myself, who trust in the revolutionary power of education believe that "learning at its most powerful could indeed liberate" (4). Education can liberate trans people. For more helpful stories and suggestions specifically for making higher education more trans inclusive, see Beemyn's (2019) edited anthology, *Trans People in Higher Education.*

Respect People's Choices About Their Own Lives

Secondly, we must respect the choices of individuals and strive to ensure that all people have the resources to make their own choices. In light of the continued attack on abortion, this may seem like a distant goal, but this is a prerequisite of equality. What many today refer to as Third Wave Feminism is founded on the premise of choice—that we should respect and trust people enough to allow them to choose what is best for their own lives. This is a pertinent concern for trans people. This is not as simple as merely saying, "I respect your choices"; rather, we must work to provide the material resources and education necessary to make choice a reality for all vulnerable populations. This point is summed up succinctly by Segal (2016, 23):

> Part of the belief system in the United States is that people have freedom of choice and that is what distinguishes Americans from citizens of so many other nations. Americans treasure their freedom and consider the United States to be the most open and free country in the world. That belief is so deep that they rarely question it. Yet is it true that all Americans are free to choose how they lead their lives? Within the framework of lawful behavior, do we have choice? To have free choice in the public domain means that: All options are open and available; Each person is aware of those options; Each person fully understands

all the options, as well as the qualifications needed to participate in the options; Each person understands the consequences, impact, and possible outcomes of all options; Sufficient resources are available for all to take advantage of all choices; Sufficient support is available to sustain a person in their choice; People have the abilities, skills, self-confidence, realistic assessment, and motivation needed to take advantage of all choices. . . . These aspects of free choice are the basis of social justice. The reality in America is that for poor, oppressed, and disenfranchised people, choice is often not a reality. The result is social injustice.

It is not enough to say people can live the way they choose, we must guarantee that people understand their options, have the resources available to take advantage of their choices, and are accepted and encouraged to live their lives in a way that works for them.

Teach and Practice Empathy

My final recommendation to improve the lives of trans men in the South, and all people, is to teach and practice empathy. Empathy moves us beyond sympathy—feeling sorry for someone—and "requires identifying oneself with another, thereby entering into the other's experience" (Segal 2016, 20). While ethics, morality, and values may be open for debate, a person's identity is not. Empathy means we listen to each other. We believe each other. We respect each other for who we are. This requires us to move beyond tolerance, and strive for acceptance and love.

I want to end this book with a similar plea for empathy as the one with which I ended my previous book (Rogers 2019b). Without empathy, we will never reach equality. I believe that education is key to spreading empathy and teaching respect for others' right to make choices about their own lives. However, while education is necessary, it is not sufficient for empathy. In addition to "traditional" sociology courses, I teach courses in social services. I tell my students each semester, "If I could wave a magic wand and give you all empathy, for all people and groups, social service courses would not be necessary." I truly believe that by listening to, and feeling with, others we can make this world more livable for everyone.

As Hochschild (2016) explains in their ethnography of the conservative political movement in Louisiana, we have constructed "empathy walls" between various groups in this country that have led us to a standstill in many ways, both socially and politically. An empathy wall "is an obstacle to deep understanding of another person, one that can make us feel indifferent or even hostile to those who hold different beliefs" (5). Empathy walls have led to much of the interpersonal prejudice and discrimination trans people face. Many people in the U.S. believe that change has occurred too quickly and have put up a wall to learning about and understanding trans people and issues.

Even within the queer community, people have stopped listening and caring for those who are different from ourselves. As Sumerau and Cragun (2018) demonstrate, while U.S. society has progressed, "the narrative of progressive social change" ignores the reality that these changes have occurred alongside tremendous continuity, especially regarding beliefs about and treatment of trans people. Unfortunately, while progressive change has made life better for some groups in this country, such as cis women, cis gay and lesbian people, and some racial minorities, these groups have been replaced "with new out-groups who have also been fighting for change and recognition for the past fifty-plus years. . . . The American moral and political landscape faced by . . . [trans] people has not changed much at all in the past fifty years, and in some ways, things have gotten worse" (Sumerau and Cragun 2018, 71).

Hochschild writes, "Our polarization, and the increasing reality that we simply don't know each other, makes it too easy to settle for dislike and contempt. . . . We, on both sides, wrongly imagine that empathy with the 'other' side brings an end to clearheaded analysis when, in truth, it's on the other side of that [empathy] bridge that the most important analysis can begin" (xi–xii). As I argued in *Conditionally Accepted,* "We must continue to dismantle the walls built to keep African American people, LGBTQ people, and immigrant people out of society and separated from the rights they are entitled to in this country. Yet, if we ignore the voices and feelings of those on the other side of the aisle, we will get nowhere. Without empathy, equality is an impossibility" (169). In sum, we must not settle for dislike or contempt; we must continue to listen, educate, and practice empathy. Dismantling empathy walls is the only way that trans people, and other oppressed groups, will gain full access to society and a life free of oppression. Although hope is extremely important, being too optimistic—to the point of ignoring continuity in light of progressive change—will lead our society to continue to leave behind the most vulnerable groups and celebrate a half-won battle. So, continue to have hope, but also continue to be persistent in demands for equality. Until all people are seen as fully human, worthy of love, and as equals in this society, we still have work to do.

Appendix
My Queer Methods

In this study I utilized queer methodology throughout the entire process, from formulating the topic of study, to creating and carrying out my methodology, to analyzing the data and writing this book. This book is intended to be intersectional, interdisciplinary, and queer. As Jane Ward (2016, 71–72) explains, "To pair the terms 'queer' and 'methodology'—the former defined by its celebrated failure to adhere to stable classificatory systems or be contained by disciplinary boundaries, and the latter defined by orderly, discipline-specific, and easily reproducible techniques—produces something of an exciting contradiction, a productive oxymoron." My hope is that my methods have produced a productive oxymoron, and that the result of my queer methods—this book—reaches an audience ready to educate themselves about queer lives in the South and become more empathic human beings.

Overall, the book is based on in-depth interviews and conversations with 51 diverse trans men across the Southeast. I personally conducted all of the interviews between January and May of 2018. I talked with each of the trans men discussed in this book for about 30 minutes to over three and a half hours; the average length of our conversations was approximately an hour and ten minutes. Clearly, these men needed to talk and had experiences that needed to be shared with a wider audience. The interviews were semi-structured and consisted of questions designed to explore a number of themes, including trans identities, passing, gender ideology, transphobia, sexual harassment and assault, and feminist consciousness. Throughout the interview process, new ideas and questions arose and were added to subsequent interviews. For instance, while I was asking respondents about the process of legally changing their names, I became very interested in their stories of how they choose their new names (I share some of these stories in Chapter 1). These stories demonstrate the self-reflection and continuous self-evaluation that is necessary for trans men; if we all were so fully self-aware, this world would be a better place.

I decided to use phone interviews because research confirms that marginalized populations, such as trans people, feel more comfortable and share more when they are allowed to remain more anonymous (McInroy 2016). Additionally, phone interviews allowed me to speak with trans men from a broader geographical area than face-to-face interviews would have allowed. As sociologists, especially queer sociologists in the South, we are faced with practical limits due to lack of funding and lower pay. While I am thankful to my university, Georgia Southern, for the funding and support I received on this project, it was in no way enough to sustain me to travel around the Southeast for an entire semester meeting the respondents. I think part of queer methodology is, and should be, acknowledging the limits that we face in our research, yet also seeing how this leads queer researchers to creativity and new findings.

The respondents were located through snowball sampling with multiple starts. First, I contacted trans men from two previous studies I conducted about drag kinging in the Southeast (Baker and Kelly 2016; Rogers 2018a). While conducting these previous studies, I came to realize the changing nature and purpose of drag kinging in the Southeast. When drag kinging began in this region of the country, and when I was attending many of the shows back in 2008 through 2011 in Columbia, South Carolina, and the surrounding areas, the majority of the drag kings were more masculine lesbian women. As I began speaking with drag kings in South Carolina in 2013 for the first study, then across the Southeast in 2017 for my second study, I started to realize that trans men now made up a large proportion of the drag kings in the region. In my article "Drag as a Resource: Trans* and Non-Binary Individuals in the Southeastern United States," which was published in *Gender & Society* in 2018, I demonstrate how trans and non-binary kings learn about their identities and find resources for gender transition through drag kinging in the Southeast. This study led me to question where else trans men in the Southeast find resources and support. I wanted to know if the stereotypical portrayals of the Southeast as transphobic and homophobic were accurate, and if so, how trans men navigated this environment. As a Southerner myself, I knew that the South was more complicated and diverse than it is often portrayed, but not how this was being navigated by trans men across the region.

The second start for my snowball sample began by reaching out to various trans men's social and support groups across the Southeast. Through some of my previous knowledge as a queer person in the region, as well as through the all-powerful Google, I was able to locate nearly 40 trans groups across the Southeast. I sent emails to each of these groups and many responded by recommending potential interviewees or putting out calls for my study at meetings and on their group's Facebook page or listserv.

Finally, I (or I should say my awesome graduate assistant, Megan) placed posters around campus at Georgia Southern and I posted a call for participants on my personal Facebook page. The call for participants read:

> I'm interested in learning more about gender identity and, more specifically, the experiences of transgender men in the South. Participants in this study must be at least 18 years of age; identify as a transgender man, transmale, transman, female-to-male (FTM), male or man (who was assigned female at birth), or some other identity that signifies transition from female to male; and currently live in the Southeast. For the purposes of this study, the Southeast includes the following states: Alabama, Arkansas, Florida, Georgia, Kentucky, Louisiana, Mississippi, North Carolina, South Carolina, Tennessee, Virginia, and West Virginia. Please let me know if you are willing to participate in this study. If so, phone interviews will be scheduled for the Spring of 2018. The phone interview should take approximately 45 minutes to 1.5 hours to complete. Participants who complete the interview will be given a $20 gift card for your time.

All respondents were also asked to share my contact information with other trans men who may be willing to participate in the study. All the interviews were recorded, transcribed, and coded.

My methods for analyzing these data were queer. They varied. They were based on specific questions and theories I had interest in. They were based on themes that emerged from the data that I hadn't even considered. They came from my own personal experiences as a trans person in the South. They came from the experiences of the men I spoke with. I analyzed the data using an approach of "cultural humility." Lombardi (2018, 75) describes it this way: "Cultural humility allows researchers to see the people they are investigating as the experts concerning their lives." I allowed my respondents to tell me what mattered to them, and how they viewed issues of gender, sexuality, prejudice, discrimination, sexual violence, etc. My respondents are experts in their own identities and lives. I choose here not to continue "the obligatory rehearsal of 'grounded theory' to describe any and all qualitative research" (Ward 2018, 61). While grounded theory played a role in this analysis, the queer methods of analysis throughout this book are much broader and more diverse than grounded theory alone can capture. Queer methods are much more empathetic, yet also messier, but I agree with others (C. Connell 2018; Ward 2018) that it is worth the messiness to really learn from others. As C. Connell (2018, 138) concludes, "I am encouraged by the reminders that the pursuit of queer research is not the *resolution* of ambivalence, contradiction, or failure in the field, but rather the *recognition*—to tolerate the uncertainty and the vulnerability, the pleasures and the pains of the work, and keep asking, keep thinking, keep writing, keep fighting in the face of it."

References

Abelson, Miriam J. 2014. "Dangerous Privilege: Trans Men, Masculinities, and Changing Perceptions of Safety." *Sociological Forum* 29, no. 3: 549–570.

———. 2016a. "'You Aren't from Around Here': Race, Masculinity, and Rural Transgender Men." *Gender, Place & Culture* 23, no. 11: 1535–1546.

———. 2016b. "Negotiating Vulnerability and Fear: Rethinking the Relationship Between Violence and Contemporary Masculinity." In *Exploring Masculinities: Identity, Inequality, Continuity, and Change*, edited by C. J. Pascoe and Tristan Bridges, 394–401. New York: Oxford University Press.

———. 2019. *Men in Place: Trans Masculinity, Race, and Sexuality in America.* Minneapolis: University of Minnesota Press.

Altemeyer, Bob, and Bruce Hunsberger. 1992. "Authoritarianism, Religious Fundamentalism, Quest, and Prejudice." *The International Journal for the Psychology of Religion* 2, no. 2: 113–133.

Anderson, Eric. 2016. "Inclusive Masculinities." In *Exploring Masculinities: Identity, Inequality, Continuity, and Change*, edited by C. J. Pascoe and Tristan Bridges, 178–187. New York: Oxford University Press.

Baker, Ashley A. (now Baker A. Rogers) and Kimberly Kelly. 2016. "Live Like a King, Y'all: Gender Negotiation and the Performance of Masculinity Among Southern Drag Kings." *Sexualities* 19, no. 1–2: 46–63.

Baker, Ashley A. (now Baker A. Rogers) and Sarah Brauner-Otto. 2015. "My Friend is Gay, but . . . The Effects of Social Contact on Christian Evangelicals' Beliefs about Gays & Lesbians." *Review of Religious Research* 57, no. 2: 239–268.

Barrett-Fox, Rebecca. 2016. *God Hates: Westboro Baptist Church, American Nationalism, and the Religious Right.* Lawrence: University Press of Kansas.

Barton, Bernadette. 2012. *Pray the Gay Away: The Extraordinary Lives of Bible Belt Gays.* New York: New York University Press.

Bauer, Patricia J., Aylin Tasdemir-Ozdes, and Marina Larkina. "Adults' Reports of Their Earliest Memories: Consistency in Events, Ages, and Narrative Characteristics Over Time." *Consciousness and Cognition* 27: 76–88.

Baunach, Dawn M., Elisabeth O. Burgess, and Courtney S. Muse. 2010. "Southern (Dis)Comfort: Sexual Prejudice and Contact with Gay Men and Lesbians in the South." *Sociological Spectrum* 30, no. 1: 30–64.

Beemyn, Genny, ed. 2019. *Trans People in Higher Education.* Albany: State University of New York Press.

Beemyn, Genny, and Sue Rankin. 2011. *The Lives of Transgender People.* New York: Columbia University Press.

Bradford, Judith, Sari L. Reisner, Julie A. Honnold, and Jessica Xavier. 2013. "Experiences of Transgender-Related Discrimination and Implications for Health: Results from the Virginia Transgender Health Initiative Study." *American Journal of Public Health* 103, no. 10: 1820–29.

Bridges, Tristan. 2014. "A Very 'Gay' Straight?: Hybrid Masculinities, Sexual Aesthetics, and the Changing Relationship between Masculinity and Homophobia." *Gender & Society* 28, no. 1: 58–82.

Bridges, Tristan, and C. J. Pascoe. 2016. "Masculinities and Post-Homophobias?" In *Exploring Masculinities: Identity, Inequality, Continuity, and Change*, edited by C. J. Pascoe and Tristan Bridges, 412–423. New York: Oxford University Press.

Brown, Trent. 2017. "On Studying Sex in the American South." In *Sex and Sexuality in Modern Southern Culture*, edited by Trent Brown, 1–25. Baton Rouge: Louisiana State University Press.

———, ed. 2017. *Sex & Sexuality in Modern Southern Culture.* Baton Rouge: Louisiana State University Press.

Carter, J. Scott, and Casey A. Borch. 2005. "Assessing the Effects of Urbanism and Regionalism on Gender-Role Attitudes, 1974–1998." *Sociological Inquiry* 75, no. 4: 548–63.

Catalano, D. Chase J. 2015. "'Trans Enough?' The Pressures Trans Men Negotiate in Higher Education." *TSQ: Transgender Studies Quarterly* 2, no. 3: 411–430.

Chatterjee, Rhitu. 2018. "A New Survey Finds 81 Percent of Women Have Experienced Sexual Harassment." *National Public Radio (NPR)*. Accessed February 2, 2019. https://www.npr.org/sections/thetwo-way/2018/02/21/587671849/a-new-survey-finds-eighty-percent-of-women-have-experienced-sexual-harassment.

Clements-Nolle, Kristen, Rani Marx, and Mitchell Katz. 2006. "Attempted Suicide among Transgender Persons: The Influence of Gender-Based Discrimination and Victimization." *Journal of Homosexuality* 51, no. 3: 53–69.

Coleman, Eli. 1981. "Developmental Stages of the Coming Out Process." *Journal of Homosexuality* 7, no. 2–3: 31–43.

Collins, Patricia Hill. 1986. "Learning from the Outsider Within: The Sociological Significance of Black Feminist Thought." *Social Problems* 33, no. 6: 14–32.

———. 2009. *Black Feminist Thought: Knowledge, Consciousness, and the Politics of Empowerment.* New York: Routledge.

Connell, Catherine. 2010. "Doing, Undoing, or Redoing Gender? Learning from the Workplace Experiences of Transpeople." *Gender & Society* 24, no. 1: 31–55.

———. 2018. "Thank You For Coming Out Today: The Queer Discomforts in In-Depth Interviewing." In *Other, Please Specify: Queer Methods in Sociology*, edited by D'Lane Compton, Tey Meadow, and Kristen Schilt, 126–139. Berkeley: University of California Press.

Connell, Raewyn. 2005. *Masculinities.* 2nd edition. Berkeley: University of California Press.

———. 2009a. *Short Introductions: Gender.* New York: Polity Press.

———. 2009b. "Accountable Conduct: 'Doing Gender' in Transsexual and Political Retrospect." *Gender & Society* 23, no. 1: 104–111.

Connell, Raewyn, and James W. Messerschmidt. 2005. "Hegemonic Masculinity: Rethinking the Concept." *Gender & Society* 19, no. 6: 829–59.

Cotten, Trystan T. 2012. *Hung Jury: Testimonies of Genital Surgery by Transsexual Men.* Oakland: Transgress Press.

Cragun, Ryan T., and J. E. Sumerau. 2015. "The Last Bastion of Sexual and Gender Prejudice? Sexualities, Race, Gender, Religiosity, and Spirituality in the Examination of Prejudice Toward Sexual and Gender Minorities." *Journal of Sex Research* 52, no. 7: 821–34.

Crenshaw, Kimberle. 1989. "Demarginalizing the Intersection of Race and Sex: A Black Feminist Critique of Antidiscrimination Doctrine, Feminist Theory and Antiracist Politics." *University of Chicago Legal Forum* 1, no. 8: 139–67.

Cromwell, Jason. 1999. *Transmen and FTMs: Identities, Bodies, Genders, and Sexualities.* Champaign: University of Illinois Press.

Davis, Georgiann. 2015. *Contesting Intersex: The Dubious Diagnosis.* New York: New York University Press.

Dawkins, Marcia Alesan. 2012. *Clearly Invisible: Racial Passing and the Color of Cultural Identity.* Waco: Baylor University Press.

Deutsch, Frances. 2007. "Undoing Gender." *Gender & Society* 21, no. 2: 106–127.

dickey, lore m., Stephanie L. Budge, Sabra L. Katz-Wise, and Michael V. Garza. 2016. "Health Disparities in the Transgender Community: Exploring Differences in Insurance Coverages." *Psychology of Sexual Orientation and Gender Diversity* 3, no. 3: 275–82.

Duck, Robert J., and Bruce Hunsberger. 1999. "Religious Orientation and Prejudice: The Role of Religious Proscription, Right-Wing Authoritarianism, and Social Desirability." *International Journal for the Psychology of Religion* 9, no. 3: 157–179.

Duggan, Lisa. 2002. "The New Homonormativity: The Sexual Politics of Neoliberalism." In *Materializing Democracy: Toward a Revitalized Cultural Politics*, edited by Russ Castronovo and Dana D. Nelson. Durham: Duke University Press.

Emerson, Michael O., and Christian Smith. 2001. *Divided by Faith: Evangelical Religion and the Problem of Race in America.* New York: Oxford University Press.

Emerson, Michael O. with Rodney Woo. 2006. *People of the Dream: Multiracial Congregations in the United States.* Princeton: Princeton University Press.

Ezzell, Matthew B. 2012. "'I'm in Control': Compensatory Manhood in a Therapeutic Community." *Gender & Society* 26, no. 2: 190–215.

———. 2016. "Healthy for Whom?—Males, Men, and Masculinity: A Reflection on the Doing (and Study) of Dominance." In *Exploring Masculinities: Identity, Inequality, Continuity, and Change*, edited by C. J. Pascoe and Tristan Bridges, 188–197. New York: Oxford University Press.

Festinger, Leon. 1957. *A Theory of Cognitive Dissonance*. Palo Alto: Stanford University Press.

Fetner, Tina. 2008. *How the Religious Right Shaped Lesbian and Gay Activism*. Minneapolis: University of Minnesota Press.

Flores, Andrew R., Jody L. Herman, Gary J. Gates, and Taylor N. T. Brown. 2016. *How Many Adults Identify as Transgender in the United States?* Los Angeles: Williams Institute.

Foucault, Michel. 1978. *The History of Sexuality, Volume 1: An Introduction*. New York: Vintage.

———. 1980. *Power/Knowledge: Selected Interviews and Other Writings, 1972–1977*. New York: Pantheon Books.

Friend, Craig T. 2009. *Southern Masculinity: Perspectives on Manhood in the South Since Reconstruction*. Athens: University of Georgia Press.

Galupo, M. Paz, Kyle S. Davis, Ashley L. Grynkiewicz, and Renae C. Mitchell. 2014. "Conceptualization of Sexual Orientation Identity among Sexual Minorities: Patterns across Sexual and Gender Identity." *Journal of Bisexuality* 14, no. 3–4: 433–456.

Garner, T. 2014. "Becoming." *TSQ: Transgender Studies Quarterly* 1, no. 1–2: 30–32.

Glenn, Evelyn Nakano. 2002. *Unequal Freedom: How Race and Gender Shaped American Citizenship and Labor*. Cambridge: Harvard University Press.

Grant, Jaime M., Lisa A. Mottet, Justin Tanis, Jack Harrison, Jody L. Herman, and Mara Keisling. 2011. "Injustice at Every Turn: A Report of the National Transgender Discrimination Survey." National Center for Transgender Equality. Accessed January 1, 2019. http://www.transequality.org/issues/resources/national-transgender-discrimination-survey-full-report.

Guignard, Florence Pasche. 2015. "A Gendered Bun in the Oven: The Gender-Reveal Party as a New Ritualization During Pregnancy." *Studies in Religion* 44, no. 4: 479–500.

Guittar, Nicholas A. 2014. *Coming Out: The New Dynamics*. Boulder: First Forum Press.

Halberstam, Jack. 1998. *Female Masculinity*. Durham: Duke University Press.

———. 2018. *Trans: A Quick and Quirky Account of Gender Variability*. Berkeley: University of California Press.

Hartke, Austen. 2018. *Transforming: The Bible & the Lives of Transgender Christians*. Louisville: Westminster John Knox Press.

Hobbs, Allyson Vanessa. 2014. *A Chosen Exile: A History of Racial Passing in American Life*. Cambridge: Harvard University Press.

Hochschild, Arlie Russell. 2016. *Strangers in Their Own Land: Anger and Mourning on the American Right*. New York: The New Press.

Holvino, Evangelina. 2008. "Intersections: The Simultaneity of Race, Gender and Class in Organization Studies." *Gender, Work and Organization* 17, no. 3: 248–277.

hooks, bell. 1994. *Teaching to Transgress: Education as the Practice of Freedom*. New York: Routledge.

Inter-American Commission on Human Rights. 2014. *An Overview of Violence Against LGBTI Persons: A Registry Documenting Acts of Violence between January 1, 2013 and March 31, 2014.* Annex—Press Release 153/14.

Jauk, Daniela. 2013. "Gender Violence Revisited: Lessons from Violent Victimization of Transgender Identified Individuals." *Sexualities* 16, no. 7: 807–825.

Jennings, Jazz. 2016. "What Jazz Jennings Wants All Trans Kids to Know." *Time.* Accessed September 18, 2018 from https://time.com/4275809/jazz-jennings-trans gender-rights/.

Johnson, Austin H. 2015. "Normative Accountability: How the Medical Model Influences Transgender Identities and Experiences." *Sociology Compass* 9, no. 9: 803–813.

———. 2016. "Transnormativity: A New Concept and Its Validation through Documentary Film about Transgender Men." *Sociological Inquiry* 86, no. 4: 465–491.

———. 2019. "Rejecting, Reframing, and Reintroducing: Trans People's Strategic Engagement with the Medicalisation of Gender Dysphoria." *Sociology of Health & Illness* 41, no. 3: 517–532.

Johnson, Colin R., Brian J. Gilley, and Mary L. Gray. 2016. "Introduction." In *Queering the Countryside: New Frontiers in Rural Queer Studies*, edited by Mary L. Gray, Colin R. Johnson, and Brian J. Gilley, 1–21. New York: New York University Press.

Johnson, E. Patrick. 2008. *Sweet Tea: Black Gay Men of the South.* Chapel Hill: The University of North Carolina Press.

Kazyak, Emily. 2012. "Midwest or Lesbian? Gender, Rurality, and Sexuality." *Gender & Society* 26, no. 6: 825–848.

Kosmin, Barry A., Ariela Keysar, Ryan Cragun, and Juhem Navarro-Rivera. 2009. *American Nones: The Profile of the No Religion Population.* Connecticut: Institute for the Study of Secularism in Society and Culture.

Lavers, Michael K. 2014. "Report: 594 LGBT people murdered in Americas during 15-month period." *Washington Blade.* Accessed August 1, 2018. https://www .washingtonblade.com/2014/12/20/report-594-lgbt-people-murdered-americas -15-month-period/.

Lombardi, Emilia. 2018. "Trans Issues in Sociology." In *Other, Please Specify: Queer Methods in Sociology*, edited by D'Lane Compton, Tey Meadow, and Kristen Schilt, 67–79. Berkeley: University of California Press.

Mahaffy, Kimberly A. 1996. "Cognitive Dissonance and Its Resolution: A Study of Lesbian Christians." *Journal for the Scientific Study of Religion* 35, no. 4: 392–402.

Manning, Jennifer E. 2018. "Membership of the 115th Congress: A Profile." *Congressional Research Service.* Accessed April 12, 2019. https://www.senate.gov/CRS pubs/b8f6293e-c235-40fd-b895-6474d0f8e809.pdf.

Mathers, Lain A. B., J. E. Sumerau, and Ryan T. Cragun. 2018. "The Limits of Homonormativity Constructions of Bisexual and Transgender People in the Post-Gay Era." *Sociological Perspectives* 61, no. 6: 934–952.

Mazzuca, Josephine. 2002. "U. S. Race Relations by Religion: The South." Accessed November 10, 2019. http://news.gallup.com/poll7234/us-race-relatios-region .south.aspx.

McDermott, Elizabeth, and Katrina Roen. 2012. "Youth on the Virtual Edge: Researching Marginalized Sexualities and Genders Online." *Qualitative Health Research* 22, no. 4: 560–570.

McInroy, Lauren B. 2016. "Pitfalls, Potentials, and Ethics of Online Survey Research: LGBTQ and Other Marginalized and Hard-to-Access Youths." *Social Work Research* 40, no. 2: 83–93.

McQueeney, Krista. 2009. "'We are God's Children, Y'all': Race, Gender, and Sexuality in Lesbian- and Gay- Affirming Congregations." *Social Problems* 56, no. 1: 151–173.

Meadow, Tey. 2018. *Trans Kids: Being Gendered in the Twenty-First Century.* Berkeley: University of California Press.

Merriam-Webster Dictionary. 2019. May 1, 2019. https://www.merriam-webster.com.

Meyer, Ilan H. 2003. "Prejudice, Social Stress, and Mental Health in Lesbian, Gay, and Bisexual Populations: Conception Issues and Research Evidence." *Psychological Bulletin* 129, no. 5: 674–697.

Miller, Lisa R., and Eric Anthony Grollman. 2015. "The Social Costs of Gender Nonconformity for Transgender Adults: Implications for Discrimination and Health." *Sociological Forum* 30, no. 3: 809–831.

Mitchell, Kimberly J., Michele L. Ybarra, and Josephine D. Korchmaros. 2014. "Sexual Harassment among Adolescents of Different Sexual Orientations and Gender Identities." *Child Abuse & Neglect* 38, no. 2: 280–295.

Mohanty, Chandra Talpade. 2003. *Feminism without Borders: Decolonizing Theory, Practicing Solidarity.* Durham: Duke University Press.

Nash, Catherine Jean. 2011. "Trans Experiences in Lesbian and Queer Space." *The Canadian Geographer* 55, no. 2: 192–207.

National Center for Transgender Equality. 2019. "ID Documents Center | Georgia." Accessed March 20, 2019. https://transequality.org/documents/state/georgia.

National Sexual Violence Resource Center (NSVRC). 2019. "Get Statistics." Accessed February 2, 2019. https://www.nsvrc.org/statistics.

Newton, Esther. 2018. *My Butch Career: A Memoir.* Durham: Duke University Press Books.

Nicolazzo, Z. 2017. *Trans in College: Transgender Students' Strategies for Navigating Campus Life and the Politics of Inclusion.* Sterling: Stylus Publishing.

Pascoe, C. J. 2007. *"Dude, You're a Fag": Masculinity and Sexuality in High School.* Berkeley: University of California Press.

Pascoe, C. J., and Tristan Bridges, eds. 2016. *Exploring Masculinities: Identity, Inequality, Continuity, and Change.* New York: Oxford University Press.

Pew Research Center. 2014. *Religious Landscape Study.* Accessed June 17, 2018. http://www.pewforum.org/religious-landscape-study/.

Pfeffer, Carla A. 2017. *Queering Families: The Postmodern Partnerships of Cisgender Women and Transgender Men.* New York: Oxford University Press.

Rape, Abuse, Incest National Network (RAINN). 2019. "Victims of Sexual Violence: Statistics." Accessed February 2, 2019. https://www.rainn.org/statistics/victims-sexual-violence.

Ray, Brett. 2015. *My Name is Brett: Truths From a Trans Christian.* CreateSpace Independent Publishing.

Reed, John Shelton. 1986. *The Enduring South: Subcultural Persistence in Mass Society.* Chapel Hill: The University of North Carollina Press.

Reynolds, Heath Mackenzie, and Zil Garner Goldstein. 2014. "Social Transition." In *Trans Bodies, Trans Selves: A Resource for the Transgender Community*, edited by Laura Erickson-Schroth, 124–154. New York: Oxford University Press.

Risman, Barbara. 2009. "From Doing to Undoing: Gender as We Know It." *Gender & Society* 23, no. 1: 81–84.

Rogers, Baker A. 2018a. "Drag as a Resource: Trans* and Non-Binary Individuals in the Southeastern United States." *Gender & Society* 32, no. 6: 889–910.

———. 2018b. "What's in a Label: The Lesbian Generational Divide." *Feminist Reflections.* https://thesocietypages.org/feminist/2018/11/16/whats-in-a-label-the -lesbian-generational-divide/.

———. 2019a. "'Contrary to All the Shit I Said': Trans Men Passing in the South." *Qualitative Sociology* 42, no.4: 639–662.

———. 2019b. *Conditionally Accepted: Christians' Perspectives on Homosexuality & Gay and Lesbian Civil Rights.* New Brunswick: Rutgers University Press.

Rowatt, Wade C., Jo-Ann Tsang, Jessica Kelly, Brooke LaMartina, Michelle Mc-Cullers, and April McKinley. 2006. "Associations Between Religious Personality Dimensions and Implicit Homosexual Prejudice." *Journal for the Scientific Study of Religion* 45, no. 3: 397–406.

Rubin, Henry. *Self-Made Men: Identity and Embodiment among Transsexual Men.* Nashville: Vanderbilt University Press.

Schilt, Kristen. 2006. "Just One of the Guys? How Transmen Make Gender Visible at Work." *Gender & Society* 20, no. 4: 465–490.

Schilt, Kristen, and Catherine Connell. 2007. "Do Workplace Gender Transitions Make Gender Trouble?" *Gender, Work and Organization* 14, no. 6: 596–618.

Schoenfeld, Jené. 2014. "Can One Really Choose? Passing and Self-Identification at the Turn of the Twenty-First Century." In *Passing Interest: Racial Passing in US Novels, Memoirs, Television, and Film, 1990–2010*, edited by Julie Nerad, 95–121. Albany: State University of New York Press.

Schrock, Douglas, and Michael Schwalbe. 2009. "Men, Masculinity, and Manhood Acts." *Annual Review of Sociology* 35, no. 1: 277–295.

Schwalbe, Michael. 2014. *Manhood Acts: Gender and the Practice of Domination.* New York: Routledge.

Segal, Elizabeth A. 2016. *Social Welfare Policy and Social Programs: A Values Perspective.* 4th edition. Boston: Cengage Learning.

Shields, Stephanie. 2008. "Gender: An Intersectionality Perspective." *Sex Roles* 59, no. 5: 301–311.

Smith, Christian, with Michael Emerson, Sally Gallagher, Paul Kennedy, and David Sikkink. 1998. *American Evangelicalism: Embattled and Thriving.* Chicago: University of Chicago Press.

Spade, Dean. 2003. "Resisting Medicine, Re/Modeling Gender." *Berkeley Women's Law Journal*, 18, no. 1: 15–37.

Stein, Arlene. 2018. *Unbound: Transgender Men and the Remaking of Identity*. New York: Pantheon Books.

Steinmetz, Katy. 2014. "The Transgender Tipping Point." *Time*. Accessed June 1, 2019. http://time.com/135480/transgender-tipping-point.

Stone, Amy L. 2018. "The Geography of Research on LGBTQ Life: Why Sociologists Should Study the South, Rural Queers, and Ordinary Cities." *Sociology Compass* 12, no. 11: 1–15.

Stop Street Harassment. 2014. *Unsafe and Harassed in Public Places: A National Street Harassment Report*. Accessed February 2, 2019. http://www.stopstreethar assment.org/our-work/nationalstudy/.

Stotzer, Rebecca L. 2009. "Violence Against Transgender People: A Review of United States Data." *Aggression and Violent Behavior* 14, no. 3: 170–179.

Stryker, Susan. 2017. *Transgender History: The Roots of Today's Revolution*. 2nd edition. New York: Seal Press.

Sumerau, J. E. 2012. "'That's What a Man Is Supposed to Do': Compensatory Manhood Acts in an LGBT Christian Church." *Gender & Society* 26, no. 3: 461–487.

Sumerau, J. E., Harry Barbee, Lain A. B. Mathers, and Victoria Eaton. 2018. "Exploring the Experiences of Heterosexual and Asexual Transgender People." *Social Sciences* 7, no. 9: 1–16.

Sumerau, J. E., and Ryan T. Cragun. 2018. *Christianity and the Limits of Minority Acceptance in America: God Loves (Almost) Everyone*. Lanham: Lexington Books.

Sumerau, J. E., Eric Anthony Grollman, and Ryan T. Cragun. 2018. "'Oh My God, I Sound Like a Horrible Person': Generic Processes in the Conditional Acceptance of Sexual and Gender Diversity." *Symbolic Interaction* 42, no. 1: 62–82.

Sumerau, J. E., and Lain A. B. Mathers. 2019. *America Through Transgender Eyes*. Lanham: Rowman & Littlefield.

The Associated Press. 2014. "Louisiana: Anti-Sodomy Law Stands." *New York Times*. Accessed May 29, 2019. https://www-nytimes-com.libez.lib.georgiasouthern .edu/2014/04/16/us/louisiana-anti-sodomy-law-stands.html.

Travers, Ann. 2018. *The Trans Generation: How Trans Kids (and Their Parents) Are Creating a Gender Revolution*. New York: New York University Press.

Wade, Lisa, and Myra Marx Ferree. 2019. *Gender: Ideas, Interactions, Institutions*. 2nd edition. New York: W. W. Norton & Company.

Ward, Jane. 2016. "Dyke Methods: A Meditation on Queer Studies and the Gay Men Who Hate It." *Women's Studies Quarterly* 44, no. 3–4: 68–88.

———. 2018. "The Methods Gatekeepers and the Exiled Queers." In *Other, Please Specify: Queer Methods in Sociology*, edited by D'Lane Compton, Tey Meadow, and Kristen Schilt, 51–66. Berkeley: University of California Press.

West, Candace, and Don H. Zimmerman. 1987. "Doing Gender." *Gender & Society* 1, no. 2: 125–151.

West, Candace, and Don H. Zimmerman. 2009. "Accounting for Doing Gender." *Gender & Society* 23, no. 1: 11–22.

Whitley, Bernard E. Jr. 2009. "Religiosity and Attitudes toward Lesbians and Gay Men: A Meta-Analysis." *The International Journal for the Psychology of Religion* 19: 21–38.

Index

About the Author

Baker A. Rogers is an Assistant Professor of Sociology at Georgia Southern University. Their research focuses on inequality, specifically examining the intersections of gender, sexuality, religion, and geographical location. Their work is published in *Qualitative Sociology* (2019), *Gender & Society* (2018), *Sexualities* (2016), *Review of Religious Research* (2016), and *Feminist Teacher* (2015). Their book *Conditionally Accepted: Christians' Perspectives on Homosexuality & Gay and Lesbian Civil Rights* was released in December 2019.

www.ingramcontent.com/pod-product-compliance
Lightning Source LLC
Chambersburg PA
CBHW050610280326
41932CB00016B/2985